SCHOLASTIC

Health & Wellbeing

- Links to *Every Child Matters* and *SEAL*
- CD-ROM includes interactive activities
- Differentiated photocopiables provided
- Easy-to-use interactive whiteboard tools

Sue Graves

AGES
5-7

Terms and conditions

Credits

Author
Sue Graves

Project Manager
Julia Stanton

Editor
Alex Albrighton

Cover Designer
Allison Parry

Series Designer
Anna Oliwa

Designer
Christina Newman (Black Dog Design)

Illustrations
Jerry Fowler, Celia Hart, Beverly Curl, Trevor Mason

CD-ROM programming and illustration
e-s-p ltd 2008

Acknowledgements

Her Majesty's Stationery Office for the use of The Green Cross Code © Crown copyright, reproduced under the terms of the Click-Use Licence C2007001963.

Material from the National Curriculum © Crown copyright. Reproduced under the terms of the Click-Use Licence C2007001963.

Every effort has been made to trace copyright holders for the works reproduced in this book, and the publishers apologise for any inadvertent omissions.

Minimum specification:
- PC with CD-ROM drive: Windows 98 or higher
- Processor: Pentium 2 (or equivalent) 1000 MHz
- RAM: 512 Mb
- Graphics card and colour monitor capable of displaying 24- bit colour graphics at a resolution of at least 1024x768 pixels.

- Mac with CD-ROM drive: OS X and above
- Processor: G3 1000 MHz
- RAM: 512 Mb
- Graphics card and colour monitor capable of displaying 24- bit colour graphics at a resolution of at least 1024x768 pixels.

Published by Scholastic Ltd
Villiers House
Clarendon Avenue
Leamington Spa
Warks. CV32 5PR
www.scholastic.co.uk

Designed using Adobe InDesign

Printed by Bell and Bain Ltd

1 2 3 4 5 6 7 8 9   8 9 0 1 2 3 4 5 6

Text © 2008 Sue Graves

© 2008 Scholastic Ltd

British Library Cataloguing-in-Publication Data
A catalogue record for this book is available from the British Library.

ISBN 978-1407-10021-0

Contents

CD-ROM contents

Unit 1 Who I am

Interactive activities:
Who are we?
Having fun outside school
My responsibilities
Photocopiables:
What I'm like (C)
What I'm like (S)
Things I like and don't like (C)
Things I like and don't like (S)
Looking after my money (C)
My special place (C)
My special place (E)
Self-evaluation: What I've learned about who I am
Photos:
My special places
Templates, cards and illustrations:
Look what I can do!
My challenge
What matters to us
My special memory
Children's booklet:
All about me

Unit 2 Feelings

Interactive activities:
Being friendly
Good resolutions
Feeling frightened
Photocopiables:
My feelings (C)
My feelings (E)

Photocopiables
C = Core
S = Support
E = Extension

I feel excited! (C)

Feeling cross (C)

Feeling cross (E)

Being kind (C)

Being kind (E)

Self-evaluation: What I've learned about feelings

Templates, cards and illustrations:

Making people feel better

Contrasting feelings

I'm not jealous!

Conflict and resolution

My friend's feelings

Cartoon characters

Children's booklet:

My feelings

Unit 3 Keeping healthy

Interactive activities:

Healthy foods

Bumps and bruises

Healthy and unhealthy

Photocopiables:

Keeping clean (C)

Keeping clean (S)

Keeping clean (E)

People who help us to stay healthy (C)

People who help us to stay healthy (E)

Noisy and quiet places (C)

Noisy and quiet places (S)

Self-evaluation: What I've learned about being healthy

Photos:

Pets

Templates, cards and illustrations:
Healthy survey
Food diary
My health plan
Children's booklet:
Healthy me

Unit 4 Keeping safe

Interactive activities:
Safe and unsafe places
Emergency!
Who can help?
Photocopiables:
Danger! (C)
Danger! (S)
The Green Cross Code (C)
Bullying is bad! (C)
Bullying is bad! (S)
Bullying is bad! (E)
Secrets (C)
Secrets (E)
Self-evaluation: What I've learned about keeping safe
Photos:
Holiday dangers
Templates, cards and illustrations:
Playground rules
Safe people
People I trust
Keep safe rules
Children's booklet:
Keeping myself safe

Unit 5 Good relationships

Interactive activities:
Caring and sharing
Moving on
Let's celebrate!
Photocopiables:
My relationships (C)
My relationships (S)
Teasing and bullying (C)
Teasing and bullying (S)
Teasing and bullying (E)
Saying goodbye (C)
Saying goodbye (S)
Self-evaluation: What I've learned about relationships
Photos:
Clothes
Celebrations
Templates, cards and illustrations:
Behaviour and relationship
Eating together
Traditional clothes
Good friendship rules
Children's booklet:
My relationships

Unit 6 Looking after our environment

Interactive activities:
Tidy up!
Recycling bins
Green spaces
Photocopiables:
Let's clean up (C)
Let's clean up (S)
Let's clean up (E)

My report (C)

My report (E)

Respect! (C)

Respect! (E)

Self-evaluation: Our environment

Templates, cards and illustrations:

Being responsible

Who's responsible?

I can help

My plan

Children's booklet:

Looking after our environment

Introduction

About the book

This book is divided into six units (listed below) which have specific links to PSHE guidelines, *Every Child Matters* objectives and the SEAL guidance.

- Who I am
- Feelings
- Keeping healthy
- Keeping safe
- Good relationships
- Looking after our environment

Each of the units contains the following elements, some of which are in the book while others are found on the CD-ROM.

- Unit planner – A framework of reference and information for teachers.

- Let's Talk – Circle time questions to introduce the unit concepts and stimulate 'thinking' about the topic.

- Twelve activities for children, concluding with two 'reflection' activities. All other resources are cross- referred from the activities.

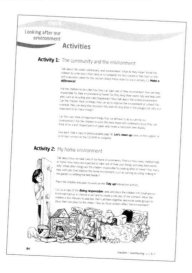

- Photocopiables – Three or four per unit, all of which are available as pdfs on the CD-ROM with differentiated photocopiables.

- Self-evaluation sheets – one for each unit.

- Interactive activities – Three activities to accompany each unit for whole-class and group discussion and completion.
- Photos – Many of the units have photos to stimulate further discussion.

- Templates, cards and illustrations – Additional resources to develop greater understanding of unit concepts, and facilitate individual and group feedback.

- Children's booklets – one for each unit to reinforce unit objectives and skill development and provide an opportunity for reflection and self-assessment. These can also be used to stimulate home involvement.

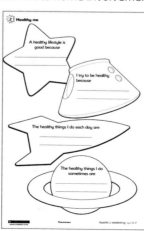
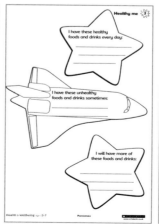
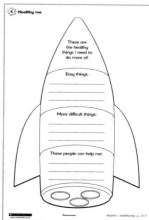

PSHE in the classroom

Setting the scene: A whole school approach

It is important to see PSHE in the classroom within the context of the ethos and environment of the whole school and its community. This is reinforced in the *Every Child Matters* legislation and the National Healthy Schools Programme. A 'Healthy' school has:
● A safe environment which supports and extends learning for all
● A supportive ethos which promotes confidence and self-reliance in all
● An extended community which is dynamic and supportive
● A 'child-centred' and integrated PSHE curriculum.

Spiral development – Revising the topics

When planning PSHE for the whole school, throughout the year there is a need to develop and revisit topics as children grow and mature. This spiral development of topics encourages children to revisit these important topics and develop skills in the PSHE areas of study which are age-appropriate, but which continue to challenge their thinking and understanding.

Let's talk – Starting with talk

Circle time is an important opportunity for children to begin an exploration of topics, question their own knowledge and articulate what they want to learn and to take away from each activity or exploration. It is an ideal way to begin each unit or activity. A range of questions has been provided for an introductory circle time discussion of each unit. Teachers are encouraged to use this opportunity to allow children to ask questions of themselves and of others, to ensure that all children remain engaged. When exploring a topic of activity, it is important to:
● Be inclusive; try to involve all children in the questioning and discussion, giving particular thought to children for whom English is an additional language.
● Redirect comments and questions, so that a number of children can respond.
● Use positive statements, and encourage children to use positive rather than negative talk (for example: *I can find out about,* rather than *I don't think I will ever be able to*).
● Summarise the discussion, sometimes during the discussion, and at the end of the session.
● Make your objectives explicit, and encourage children to do the same.

Getting involved – Using children's own work

It is important that children see themselves at the centre of the PSHE topics and have the opportunity to relate each topic to their own lives, both now and in the future. It is therefore suggested throughout the activities that children talk about and illustrate their responses to questions and comments and that these verbal and illustrated responses are shared with their peers and throughout the school, and that non-judgemental reactions from others are solicited and discussed. These personalised responses will also give teachers insights into children's thinking and perceptions.

Reflection – Questions and prompts

Reflecting on learning and group or class interaction regularly, at the end of sessions or units, is helpful to both the teacher and the children. It give teachers an opportunity to understand how children tackled the task, the strategies they used, how they interacted in small or large groups and what they think they achieved; it also allows children the opportunity to articulate what they achieved, how they worked individually or in groups and what they still want to achieve. Questions and prompts such as these can focus on the task, the strategies, the group dynamics etc and can be aimed at individual and/or group reflection:

● What strategies did you use during the activity?
● Did you achieve your goal?
● Did you get better at anything?
● Do you understand the topic better?
● Did you find it useful to work with a partner/group?
● How well did your group work?
● Could your group work better in the future?
● How do you feel about the topic?

Evaluation and assessment

The purpose of evaluating and assessing children's learning is to plan for continued skill and personal development. Where possible, both children and teachers should be involved in the assessment process, and this should include both informal and formal assessment. There are many opportunities to informally assess children's work and contributions throughout the activities. Extending this assessment to interpersonal and behavioural skills will help children become self-confident and increase their maturity. Children can use the following type of continuum to self-evaluate or peer-evaluate interpersonal and behavioural skills:

I encourage others to give their opinions on the topic.

I listen to others.

Child A participates in group discussions.

About the series

Health & Wellbeing is a comprehensive multimedia resource that combines the requirements of *Every Child Matters* and the guidelines for PSHE and citizenship into a manageable programme of work. It is designed to enable teachers to engage in these topics throughout the primary school years.

Health & Wellbeing (ages 4-5) Foundation units	Early Learning Goals (Personal, social and emotional development)	Every Child Matters	SEAL
This is me	Be confident to try new activities, initiate ideas and speak in a familiar group Have a developing awareness of their own needs, views and feelings and be sensitive to those of others	Enjoy and achieve	Good to be me Going for goals! Changes
All the things I need	Have a developing awareness of their own needs, views and feelings and be sensitive to those of others	Enjoy and achieve Achieve economic well-being	Changes
My feelings	Respond to significant experiences, showing a range of feelings when appropriate Be confident to try new activities, initiate ideas and speak in a familiar group	Enjoy and achieve	New beginnings Getting on and falling out Good to be me
Thinking about others	Have a developing awareness of their own needs, views and feelings and be sensitive to those of others Understand that people have different needs, views, cultures and beliefs, that need to be treated with respect	Enjoy and achieve	New beginnings Getting on and falling out Good to be me
My body	Dress and undress independently and manage their own personal hygiene	Be healthy	Changes
Healthy me	Dress and undress independently and manage their own personal hygiene	Be healthy	Changes
Be safe!	Consider the consequences of their words and actions for themselves and others	Stay safe	Say no to bullying
My friends and family	Form good relationships with adults and peers Work as part of a group or class, taking turns and sharing fairly	Make a positive contribution	Getting on and falling out Say no to bullying Relationships
Playtime	Form good relationships with adults and peers Consider the consequences of their words and actions for themselves and others	Make a positive contribution	Getting on and falling out Say no to bullying Relationships
My community	Have a developing awareness of their own needs, views and feelings, and be sensitive to those of others Have a developing respect for their own cultures and beliefs and those of others Work as part of a group or class, taking turns and sharing fairly	Make a positive contribution	Changes
Right and wrong	Understand what is right and wrong and why Consider the consequences of their words and actions for themselves and others Work as part of a group or class, taking turns and sharing fairly	Make a positive contribution	Changes

Health & Wellbeing (ages 5-7) KS1 units	National Curriculum	Every Child Matters	SEAL
Who I am	Developing confidence and responsibility and making the most of their abilities	Enjoy and achieve Achieve economic well-being	Good to be me Going for goals! Changes
Feelings	Developing confidence and responsibility and making the most of their abilities	Enjoy and achieve	New beginnings Getting on and falling out Good to be me
Keeping healthy	Developing a healthy, safer lifestyle	Be healthy	Changes
Keeping safe	Developing a healthy, safer lifestyle	Stay safe	Say no to bullying Changes
Good relationships	Developing good relationships and respecting the differences between people	Make a positive contribution	Getting on and falling out Say no to bullying Relationships
Looking after our environment	Preparing to play a role as active citizens	Make a positive contribution	Changes

Health & Wellbeing (ages 7-9) Lower KS2 units	National Curriculum	Every Child Matters	SEAL
All about me	Developing confidence and responsibility and making the most of their abilities Developing good relationships and respecting the differences between people	Enjoy and achieve Make a positive contribution	Good to be me Going for goals! Changes Relationships
My feelings	Developing confidence and responsibility and making the most of their abilities Preparing to play an active role as citizens	Enjoy and achieve Make a positive contribution	Getting on and falling out Say no to bullying Good to be me Relationships
Healthy me	Developing a healthy, safer lifestyle	Be healthy Make a positive contribution	Changes Relationships
My safety	Developing a healthy, safer lifestyle	Stay safe Make a positive contribution	Say no to bullying Going for goals!
My relationships	Developing good relationships and respecting the differences between people	Make a positive contribution Enjoy and achieve	New beginnings Getting on and falling out Say no to bullying Relationships
My community and environment	Preparing to play a role as active citizens Developing confidence and responsibility and making the most of their abilities	Make a positive contribution	Changes Relationships

Health & Wellbeing (ages 9-11) Upper KS2 units	National Curriculum	Every Child Matters	SEAL
Discovering myself	Developing confidence and responsibility and making the most of their abilities Developing good relationships and respecting the differences between people Preparing to play a role as active citizens	Enjoy and achieve Make a positive contribution Stay safe	Good to be me Going for goals! New beginnings Changes Relationships
Good days and bad days	Developing confidence and responsibility and making the most of their abilities Developing good relationships and respecting the differences between people Preparing to play an active role as citizens	Enjoy and achieve Make a positive contribution	New beginnings Getting on and falling out Say no to bullying Going for goals! Good to be me Relationships
A healthy lifestyle	Developing a healthy, safer lifestyle Developing confidence and responsibility and making the most of their abilities	Be healthy Make a positive contribution	Changes Good to be me Relationships
Am I safe?	Developing a healthy, safer lifestyle Developing confidence and responsibility and making the most of their abilities	Stay safe Make a positive contribution	Say no to bullying Going for goals!
Relationships	Developing good relationships and respecting the differences between people Preparing to play an active role as citizens	Make a positive contribution Enjoy and achieve	New beginnings Getting on and falling out Say no to bullying Going for goals! Relationships
My community and environment	Preparing to play a role as active citizens Developing confidence and responsibility and making the most of their abilities Developing good relationships and respecting the differences between people	Make a positive contribution Enjoy and achieve	Changes Relationships

How to use the CD-ROM

System requirements

Minimum specification:
- PC with CD-ROM drive: Windows 98 or higher
- Processor: Pentium 2 (or equivalent) 1000 MHz
- RAM: 512 Mb
- Graphics card and colour monitor capable of displaying 24-bit colour graphics at a resolution of at least 1024x768 pixels.

- Mac with CD-ROM drive: OS X and above
- Processor: G3 1000 MHz
- RAM: 512 Mb
- Graphics card and colour monitor capable of displaying 24-bit colour graphics at a resolution of at least 1024x768 pixels.

Getting started

The *Health & Wellbeing* CD-ROM program should auto-run when you insert the CD-ROM into your CD drive. If it does not, use My Computer to browse the contents of the CD-ROM and click on the *Health & Wellbeing* icon.

From the start-up screen there are four options: Click **Credits** to view a list of acknowledgements. If you would like to register an interest in the series, click on **Registration** and follow the prompt. You must then click on **Terms and conditions** to read the terms and the licence conditions. If you agree to these terms then click **Continue**: this will take you to the **Main menu**.

Main menu

Each of the six *Health & Wellbeing* units contains up to six different types of resource, which can be accessed as follows:
- Firstly click on the links to access the six *Health & Wellbeing* units.
- Click on **Interactive activities** to view or complete any interactive activity provided.
- Click on **Photocopiables** to view and print the photocopiable resources.
- Click on **Photos** to view and print these resources for some units.
- Click on **Templates, cards and illustrations** to view or print these pdf resources.
- Click on **Children's booklet** to view or print this 'reflection' resource.

Interactive activities

Each of the units has three interactive activities, which are referenced in the unit text. It is suggested that the interactives be viewed on an interactive whiteboard, a computer screen or a data projector and shared with the whole class for discussion in the first instance. When an activity has been completed it is checked by clicking on the **Check answers** button. Any incorrect answers are returned to their original position by clicking on the **Try again** button which gives children the opportunity to correct initial incorrect responses. To revisit the activity, click on the **Back** button.

Photocopiable resources

To view or print the photocopiable resource pages (photocopiables, templates, cards, illustrations and children's booklets), click on the required title on the list. To view photocopiables or templates as a full page, click **Actual size** and then the page icon with four arrows around it, at the top of the screen. To print the selected resource select **Print**. To return to the **Menu**, click **Back**.

Viewing and printing photos

Photos initially appear in a frame with whiteboard tools. To see the photo at full screen, click on the **Actual size** button. To print an image, click on the **Print** button. To navigate between images, use the **Next** and **Previous** buttons.

Whiteboard tools

Four tools have been provided for annotating photos and templates: a pen, highlighter, speech bubble and eraser. The tools will continue to be available if the photograph or template is displayed, or can be minimised if required. To show the tools palette again, click on the **Tools** icon.

CD navigation

- **Back:** click to return to the previous screen.
- **Help:** click to go to **How to use this CD-ROM**.
- **Home:** click to return to the **Main menu**.
- **Quit:** click to close the program.

Technical support

For all technical support queries, please phone Scholastic Customer Services on 0845 603 9091.

Unit planner

Aims of the unit

Knowing who we are and developing self-awareness are important skills for individual development. The aim of this unit is to develop the children's understanding of themselves, allowing them the opportunity to explore different aspects of their characters, their likes and dislikes, and their opinions. It also aims to make the child aware that appearances are only one aspect of a human being, and that how we behave towards others also determines our personalities.

> **Key concept**
> Understanding who I am and becoming self-aware.

Learning outcomes

By the end of this unit:

● All the children should be able to explain who they are (including giving their full name and age) and be able to describe their appearance and aspects of their personality (happy, funny, kind, shy and so on). They should also be able to identify things they can and can't do, and have a notion about what they would like to achieve in the near future.

● Most should be able to express opinions about what they like and don't like, and give reasons for these. They should also be aware of having responsibilities to themselves, their homes, their school and the community.

● Some may be able to express long-term future ambitions and skills they would like to learn. They will also be able to assess their characters in simple terms and make judgements about aspects that they would like to improve.

Curriculum links

PSHE
● Developing confidence and responsibility and making the most of their abilities

Every Child Matters
● Enjoy and achieve
● Achieve economic well-being

SEAL themes
● Good to be me
● Going for goals!
● Changes

Science
● Variation and classification: pupils should be taught to recognise similarities and differences between themselves and others and to treat others with sensitivity.

Maths
● Processing, representing and interpreting data

> **Vocabulary**
> Achievements, money, savings, likes, dislikes, challenges, goals, responsibilities, memories, changing, improving

Who I am

Organisation

The activities in this unit may be worked through in the order in which they appear or in any order to suit your ongoing planning. All of the activities are introduced as part of whole-class teaching. The follow-up activities include a range of individual, paired, small-group and whole-class work.

Resources

You will need the following resources to complete the activities in this unit:

Core photocopiable pages
Page 25 What I'm like
Page 26 Things I like and don't like
Page 27 My special place
Page 28 Self-evaluation sheet

CD-ROM

Interactive activities:
- Who are we?
- Having fun outside school
- Responsibilities

Photocopiables:
- What I'm like (support)
- Things I like and don't like (support)
- Looking after my money (core)
- My special place (extension)

Plus core photocopiables as above

Photos:
- My special places

Templates, cards and illustrations:
- Look what I can do!
- My challenge
- What matters to us
- My special memory

Children's booklet:
- All about me

Evaluation

The self-evaluation sheet and children's booklet have been designed to allow the children to assess how much they have learned about themselves during this unit. It is suggested that the child responds to the evaluation by either drawing or writing answers according to his or her ability. Some guidance from an adult helper may be necessary.

Watch points

Be aware, as you progress through the unit, that some children may have negative attitudes towards themselves and others for whatever reasons. Be ready to point out positives, especially when children are asked to identify things they are good at and things they have achieved.

Let's talk

Circle time and thinking activities

These questions will get the children thinking and talking about all the things that contribute to making them who they are. It is important to encourage the children not simply to think about what they look like or what their name is, but to focus instead on what they are like as people.

1 How do people know you? Does everyone know your name? How did you get your first name? Do you like your name? What are your favourite names?

2 What are you like as a person? What would your family and friends say you were like? What do you like best about yourself? What would you like to improve?

3 What things can you do? What things can you do that others may not be able to do? Who showed you how to do these things? What things do you find hard? How do you think you could get better?

4 What challenges do you face? What do you want to learn how to do? Why? What do you want to be when you are older? What do you want to be like? Who do you most admire? Why?

5 What things do you do outside school? Do you belong to any special clubs? Do you do any sporting activities? Why are these activities good for you? Do you enjoy them?

6 What are your favourite things? What things don't you like? Are there times when you have to do things you don't like? What do you do at these times?

7 Are there things that you are responsible for? Do you get pocket money? How do you look after it? Do you always remember to do things you have been asked to do? What makes you forget?

8 What things are important to you? Why are they important to you? What things do you think are unimportant? Does everyone agree?

9 Do you have a special place that you like to go to? What makes this place special? Do you go there on your own or with your friends? What do you do?

10 What is your earliest memory? How many of you can remember your first day at school? Can you remember your last birthday? Do you think all

Activities

Activity 1: Who am I?

I am unique

I am good
at tennis

Everyone is special and unique. There is not another one of us anywhere in the world. (If there are identical twins in class, point out that although they look the same they are still two different people!)

Ask the children to think about how people know us. Point out that when we first meet people they know us by how we look, and then by our name. Find out if all the children know their whole names, including their middle and family names. Explain that our names are very important to us.

Now talk about the children's parents or carers. Talk about how children often call carers by their first names, but usually call parents by called names such as Mum and Dad. Why do the children think this is so? Extend this to thinking about what children call their grandparents, aunts, uncles and so on.

Invite individual children to try the **Who are we?** interactive activity. They need to work out which name belongs to which person by a process of elimination.

Ask the children to draw a picture of themselves on a sheet of paper and to write their names, ages and something important about themselves underneath. Provide help words on the board as necessary. Display this work on the wall under the heading *Hello. We are Class 1!* (Keep these pictures for activity 11 **Changing and improving**.)

Activity 2: What I'm like

Encourage the children to talk about what they are like as people. Do they think they are kind, good fun, friendly? Point out that although people notice what we look like when we first meet them, it is what we are like inside that really matters.

Ask some of the children to write down three or four words that describe themselves on a piece of paper, and to keep them hidden. Invite other children to describe these children in a single word. (Be sensitive to those who might find this difficult.) See how many of the descriptions correspond.

Provide the children with copies of photocopiable page 25 **What I'm like** (core) or the support version on the CD-ROM. Ask them to think about what they are like as people, not what they look like.

Extension
Invite the children to draw a picture of their best friend – either from school or home. They should label their drawings and write a brief character description. Select children to show their finished work to the others at the end of the session.

Activity 3: Look what I can do!

Talk about all the things that the children can do. Try to encompass as many different types of achievement as possible, such as academic, cultural, sporting and personal goals. Remember that some children may not have a lot of self-esteem and may be unable or unwilling to list their achievements. Be ready to highlight their personal achievements – for example, *Mark is always helpful.*

Make a class achievement display using the four headings: *Academic, Creative* (art, music), *Sport* and *Personal* (home and community). Children can draw something they are good at to add to the display. Make sure they are identified on their drawing, as this will help discussion.

Invite children to act out an achievement of which they are particularly proud. The rest of the class must guess what it is. Remind the children that every achievement, no matter how small, is significant.

Give each child a copy of the **Look what I can do!** template. Encourage them to write or draw things that they can do in the petals of the flower. Cut out the flowers and add them to your class achievement display.

Activity 4: My challenges and goals

Introduce this activity by asking the children to think about all the things they do at school. What are their favourite things? What do they least like doing? Ask them to give reasons for their choices. Do they, for example, not like doing some things because they are difficult?

Discuss the challenges that the children face at school. Invite them to think of their own challenges and how they plan to achieve them. For example – *I think reading is difficult, but I am going to try really hard so that I get better at it.* Extend this by asking them to think of challenges they have outside school and how they propose to achieve those.

Using the **My challenge** template, ask the children to write down a challenge or goal they'd like to achieve and how they think they can achieve it. Create a display with the hot-air balloons resting in a field. As children achieve all or part of their challenges, the balloons can float up into the sky!

Extension
Ask the children to think of something they have recently found hard, but which they have managed to achieve. Encourage them to draw themselves taking the challenge and to write a few simple sentences to describe what they did.

Health & **Wellbeing** ages **5-7**

Activity 5: Having fun outside school

Ask the children to talk about activities they do outside school, in the evenings and at weekends. Do they belong to clubs such as Rainbows, Beavers, Cubs or Brownies? How many take part in sporting activities? Encourage the children to share their personal experiences with the others. With the whole class, try the **Having fun outside school** interactive activity.

Are there any other activities that the children would like to do? Point out that taking part in activities such as sport and dancing all help to promote a healthy lifestyle. Talk about the outcomes of the activities, such as getting fit, meeting people, having fun and using your talents. (Be aware that children may not be able to take part in activities because of financial constraints.)

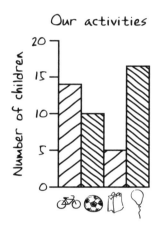

Take a straw poll to find out which activities the children take part in. Decide on relevant labels and make a class graph of their participation in activities outside school. Display the graph with other work completed in this unit.

Extension
Spend time talking to the children about things they'd like to do in the future to have fun. Which sports would they like to develop or learn? Which clubs would they like to join? Ask them to write two or three sentences on this subject and to complete their work with a drawing of themselves participating in the activities as adults.

Activity 6: Things I like and don't like

Explain to the children that everyone has different likes and dislikes. Find out what they like and dislike – their favourite and least liked school activities, toys, games, books, TV programmes and so on. Encourage the children to give reasons for their decisions. Discuss choices that the children disagree on, but remind them not to make personal comments about other children's preferences. Everyone is entitled to their own opinion.

Place the children into groups. Ask each group to think about an activity they enjoy and one they don't enjoy. Agree rules for deciding on an activity that they will present as a role play to the rest of the class. Allow them time to practise. Can the others guess what is being mimed? Do they, too, like or dislike the activities being mimed?

Display photocopiable page 27 **Things I like and don't like** on the whiteboard and discuss and complete the activity as a group. Ask another class to also complete it and compare the two.

Extension
Provide children with their own copy of photocopiable page 27 **Things I like and don't like** (core) or the support version on the CD-ROM. Ask them to fill in the sheet and to choose something that they particularly like or dislike.

Activity 7: My responsibilities

Show the **My responsibilities** interactive activity on the whiteboard. Ask the children what is meant by having responsibilities. What responsibilities do they have in school or at home? Discuss each responsibility with the children as the activity is being completed.

What are the children personally responsible for? Are they, for example, responsible for looking after their pocket money by saving some or buying the things they want? Do they have to do chores in the house or garden? Are they responsible for keeping their shoes clean?

Extend this to exploring what responsibilities they have in the community – for example, they are responsible for behaving appropriately by being respectful to other people, not damaging property, and making sure they help to keep communal areas free of litter. Compile a list of responsibilities under the headings of *Home, School* and *Community*. Children can then complete the interactive activity in pairs.

Extension
Invite the children to complete the **Looking after my money** photocopiable. Talk about what things they expect to have to save for in the future – for example, a car or house. How will they save for these things?

Activity 8: Things that matter to me

Find out what things matter to the children at school, at home and in the community. Make some suggestions to get the discussion started – for example, children might worry about how well they do at school, or how much they achieve in outside activities. They may also have wider concerns, such as the damage caused by pollution. Allow time for the children to express and identify their concerns. Remember to emphasise that all suggestions are useful.

Place the children into pairs to discuss the things that matter to them. Encourage them to think about as wide a range of things as possible. As they work, remind the children to listen while others speak and to wait their turn patiently without interrupting. Check how each pair is negotiating and interacting.

Give each pair a copy of the **What matters to us** template. Ask them to list the things that matter at school and in the community, and then discuss and record what they think they can do about each issue. One child should act as a scribe, and the other as a spokesperson to tell the others what they have written.

Activity 9: My special places

Show the children the **My special places** photos, then talk about their own special places – places where they like to play, read, or simply daydream. These may be dens in the garden or yard, places in or around home, a relative's house, or a favourite holiday location. Which are their favourite special places? Encourage the children to explain what is particularly special about these places. Have they always been special to them or are they new finds?

Now ask the children to think about the future. What special places would they like to have? Some, for example, may want their own homes; some may want their own rooms. Give all the children an opportunity to express their opinions.

Provide the children with copies of photocopiable page 27 **My special place** (core) or the extension version on the CD-ROM and ask them to complete it individually. At the end of the session, choose children to share their work with the others. How many chose the same special place?

Activity 10: My favourite memories

Check that the children understand the meaning of the word 'memory'. What are the their earliest memories? How old were they? Are the memories happy or sad? Do the children think about them often?

What are the children's memories about school? Can they all remember their first day? How did they feel? Did they feel excited, scared or worried? Encourage the children to talk about these earliest memories of school life. Now ask them to think about their other memories – for example, favourite holidays, exciting presents or a special day out. What can they remember about these things? How do they feel when they think about them?

Give each child a copy of the **My special memory** template. Ask them to draw their memory and then to write one or two sentences explaining it. Use the drawings to create a display entitled *Our memories*. The ideas could be developed into literacy activities later on, such as writing poems or descriptive recounts.

Activity 11: Changing and improving

Help the children to begin to reflect on what they have learned during this unit – about how they see themselves and others, and how they might like to improve or change something about themselves.

Hand out the papers the children completed during activity 1 **Who am I?** Allow them time to read through what they wrote. Ask the children if they now think that those details tell us enough about who we are. What other things are important when we are finding out about people?

Invite the children to talk about what they have learned about themselves during this unit. Have their opinions changed? Do they see others differently now? Explain that, as they grow older and change, they will keep learning more and more about themselves.

Now ask the children what things they would like to improve about themselves. What things would they like to change? What is important? How do they think they can improve or change things about themselves? Do they think it will be easy or hard?

Activity 12: Looking forward

Emphasise to the children that learning about ourselves is an ongoing process. Recap what the children talked about in the previous activity. What have they learned about themselves, their friends and their families?

Now ask the children to look forward to the future. What things do they want to achieve now? What do they want to achieve later on – for example, in junior school? These 'challenges' or goals could be school- and home-based. Discuss different types of goals – improving behaviour, learning a new skill, participating more with others, providing help for others, improving their health or fitness, doing different things and having more fun.

Invite children to choose one or two goals they want to achieve and to write them in a star shape. Incorporate these onto a blue background to create an *Our futures* class display.

Children can now complete the self-evaluation sheet and/or the children's booklet.

What I'm like

Write a sentence about yourself to answer these questions.

How do you help others at home? _____

_____

_____

_____

When are you helpful at school? _____

_____

_____

_____

What have you done that you are proud of? _____

_____

_____

_____

What is your special skill? _____

_____

_____

_____

Things I like and don't like

I like these things:

- _____
- _____
- _____
- _____
- _____

I like _____ best of all.

I don't like:

- _____
- _____
- _____
- _____
- _____

I don't like _____ at all!

Help words

football   swimming   reading   writing   maths   PE
cabbage   fruit   carrots   meat   fish   ice cream
homework   playing   films   friends   holidays   bed

My special place

Draw your special place here:

Why is it special?

This place is special because _____

_____

What do you do in your special place?

_____

_____

Help words
think   play   shout   read   daydream   listen

What I've learned about who I am

Name _____

This is who I am

_____

_____

_____

This is what I can do

_____

_____

_____

This is what I learned about myself

_____

_____

_____

This is what I can do now

_____

_____

_____

Unit planner

Aims of the unit

Many children find it hard to identify how others are feeling from their facial expressions or from their body language. This can result in conflict and misunderstandings, which can make social interaction difficult. The aim of this unit is to help children analyse their own feelings in different situations and then, by using this knowledge, develop an understanding of other people's feelings to improve social harmony at home, in school and outside in the wider community.

> **Key concept**
> Being aware of our own and others' feelings.

Learning outcomes

By the end of this unit:

● All the children should understand how their feelings and other people's feelings change according to circumstances. They will be able to identify a range of feelings in themselves.

● Most should be able to identify how people are feeling from observing facial expressions and general body language. They will be able to develop strategies for helping friends or family members who are unhappy to feel better.

● Some should develop a deeper understanding of how people's feelings affect their behaviour. In conflict situations, they will be able to resolve most commonly occurring issues in a non-aggressive way.

Curriculum links

PSHE
● Developing confidence and responsibility and making the most of their abilities
Every Child Matters
● Enjoy and achieve
SEAL themes
● New beginnings
● Getting on and falling out
● Good to be me
PE
● Knowledge and understanding of fitness and health: pupils should be taught to recognise and describe how their bodies feel during different activities.

> **Vocabulary**
> Feelings, safe, happy, sad, calm, relaxed, jealous, excitement, grief, friendly, kind, cross, conflict, resolution

Unit 2

Feelings

Organisation
The activities in this unit may be worked through in the order in which they appear or in any order to suit your ongoing planning. All of the activities are introduced as part of whole-class teaching. The follow-up activities include a range of individual, paired, small-group and whole-class work.

Resources
You will need the following resources to complete the activities in this unit:

Core photocopiable pages
Page 38 My feelings
Page 39 Feeling cross
Page 40 Being kind
Page 41 Self-evaluation sheet

CD-ROM

Interactive activities:
- Being friendly
- Good resolutions
- Feeling frightened

Photocopiables:
- My feelings (extension)
- I feel excited! (core)
- Feeling cross (extension)
- Being kind (extension)

Plus core photocopiables as above

Templates, cards and illustrations:
- Making people feel better
- Contrasting feelings
- I'm not jealous! cards
- Conflict and resolution cards
- My friend's feelings
- Cartoon characters

Children's booklet:
- My feelings

Evaluation
The self-evaluation sheet and children's booklet have been designed to allow the children to assess how much they have learned about their feelings during this unit. It is suggested that the child responds to the evaluation by either drawing or writing answers according to his or her ability. Some guidance from an adult helper may be necessary.

Watch points
Be aware that some children in the class may be experiencing difficulties at home or at school and feelings may be a little raw – for example, after a recent bereavement, divorce or house move. It is suggested that where this is an issue, the teacher moderates suggestions in the activities accordingly or places children in adult-supported groups to work through some of the tasks.

Let's talk

Circle time and thinking activities

These questions will get the children thinking and talking about their own feelings and those of other people.

1 What sort of different feelings can you think of? How are you feeling today? What is making you feel this way?

2 How do you generally feel when you are at school? How do you generally feel when you are at home? Why? What makes you feel really happy? What makes you feel sad? What do you do when you feel sad?

3 When do you feel calm and relaxed? When you go to bed at night? When you are on holiday? How does it feel to be calm and relaxed?

4 Have you ever felt jealous of someone? What did you feel jealous about? Did it feel nice or horrible? What did you do to stop feeling jealous? Did it work?

5 What things make you feel excited? Why? How do you feel when you are excited? Do you find it hard to sit still or concentrate? Why do you think this is?

6 Do you think you are friendly? What do you say or do to show you are being friendly? Can you think of someone who is always friendly? What do they do that makes them a friendly person?

I'm scared   I'm cross

She's friendly

We're happy   I'm sad

FEELINGS

7 What makes you cross? How do you feel when you are cross? How do you behave? Do you think it is nice to be cross with other people? Who gets cross with you? Why? How could you stop them getting cross with you?

8 Who do you argue with? What about? How do you think you both feel during an argument? What is the best way to resolve an argument? Do you always make friends after arguing with someone?

9 How many of you try to be kind to other people and to animals? Is it important to be kind to others? Why? What do you say or do to show you are being kind? Who is kind to you? What do they do?

10 How many of you have ever felt frightened? What made you frightened? Who helped you? What did they do to stop you feeling frightened? Is it sometimes fun to feel frightened?

Activities

Activity 1: How do you feel?

Introduce this unit by asking the children what feelings are. Are feelings important? Why? How do the children feel at the moment? Point out that our feelings are the moods we are in at one time. Ask the children to make a short list of the feelings they typically feel. (Keep these lists for activity 11 **Different feelings**.)

Now ask the children if they think people can tell how they are feeling simply by looking at their facial expressions. Choose children to come to the front. Whisper a feeling to them and ask them to show that feeling on their faces for the others to guess. How many children could identify the feelings easily? How many found it hard? Did the children find it easy to show their feelings on their faces? Explain that it is sometimes hard to spot how people are feeling just by looking at their expressions. We often need to look for other clues, such as how they are standing, sitting or even speaking to others.

Provide the children with copies of photocopiable page 38 **My feelings** (core) or the extension version on the CD-ROM. Ask them to draw their faces looking happy, sad, cross and frightened and to write down what makes them feel like this.

Activity 2: Happy and sad

Extend the work done in activity 1 by asking the children if they recall what made their friends happy or sad. Did the children often choose the same things? Ask the children to imagine certain situations as follows:

- *If your friend fell over, how do you think they would feel?*
- *If your friend's pet died, how do you think they would feel?*
- *If your friend got a brand new bike for their birthday, would they feel happy or sad?*

Point out that even if we aren't experiencing the feelings ourselves, we can imagine how others might be feeling by putting ourselves in their place. This helps us to understand our friends better and helps us to understand their behaviour at certain times.

Ask the children to imagine that their friend is sad because their pet dog is ill. What could they do to make them feel better? Children can record their ideas on the **Making people feel better** template. Display the completed sheets with the heading *This is how we help our friends if they feel sad*.

Our extended families

Activity 3: Feeling calm and relaxed

Ask the children what it feels like to be calm and relaxed. When do they feel like this? Are there times at home or school when they do not feel calm – during school tests for example? Do they find it hard to think properly when they feel like this? Encourage the children to think about strategies for dealing with these feelings.

In the school hall, invite the children to find a space and to lie down full length on their backs. Ask them to tense their bodies as much as they can and to notice how they feel. Now ask them to relax their bodies very slowly. How heavy do their arms and legs feel? How has their breathing slowed down? Remind them to focus on these things as they relax. Allow a few minutes for the children to experience this calmness, before asking them to roll slowly onto their sides and then sit and stand up. Talk about how they feel. Point out that relaxing in this way when they feel worried can make them feel calm. Even small steps such as slowing down their breathing can make them feel calmer in tense situations.

Using the **Contrasting feelings** template, ask the children to write down how they felt when they were tense, and how they felt after doing the relaxation exercises.

Activity 4: I'm not jealous!

Show the **I'm not jealous!** cards on the whiteboard and ask the children to identify the emotions shown. Talk about what it means to feel jealous. Have they ever felt jealous or envied someone? Why did they feel jealous? How did they deal with those feelings? Did anyone help them to overcome their feelings? What did they do?

Cut up a copy of the **I'm not jealous!** cards. Place the children into four groups and give each group a card. The children need to identify who is feeling jealous in the picture and talk about how they could resolve the problem and make everyone feel better. They can then develop a role play based on the situation to present to the rest of the class. Discuss each role play and invite the other groups to suggest additional ways to deal with each situation.

Extension
Children could record a short 'I feel lucky because...' statement onto tape.

Activity 5: Excitement

Discuss with the children the things that make them feel excited. Special treats or outings? Birthdays or special festivals? Make a class list on the board for children to refer to later.

Ask the children to describe how they feel inside when they are excited. Do they feel as if they have butterflies in their tummies? Do they feel a little sick? How many children find it hard to concentrate when they feel excited about something else?

Now talk about what other people see when we are excited. How might someone's face look if they are excited? Invite two or three children to think about something that excites them and then to show this emotion on their faces. Children could collect photos of 'excited' faces and make a collage.

Ask the children to recall occasions when they felt particularly excited – refer to the class list if necessary. Invite them to complete the ***I feel excited!*** photocopiable. They can write down why each occasion made them feel so excited on the back of the sheet.

Activity 6: Being friendly

Talk to the children about being friendly to each other. How can they show they are friends with someone? What sorts of things do friends do? What sorts of things are not friendly?

Ask the children about when they first started school. Did they make friends straight away or did it take a little time to get to know each other? Remind the children that some people are shyer than others and that they may find it harder to make friends. However, they can help shy people by including them where possible.

Invite adults such as grandparents, teaching assistants and your headteacher to come into the classroom and share their experiences of making friends at school. The children can compose questions to ask the adults prior to the visit. Afterwards, compare the adults' experiences with the children's own. How were they different? How were they similar? Children can also talk to their parents or carers about how easy they found it to make new friends on their first day at school

Invite children, working in pairs, to try the ***Being friendly*** interactive activity.

Extension
Ask the children to make a hand of friendship. They should draw around their own hand and then write a thing that good friends do on each finger.

Activity 7: Feeling cross

Ask the children what makes them feel cross. Other people or difficult situations? Encourage the children to think of times when they felt cross. Ask them to share their personal experiences with the others.

Provide the children with a small mirror each. Ask them to show an angry face. How does it look? How does it feel?

Now talk about finding ways of reducing feelings of anger. How can people stop feeling cross and help themselves to calm down? Examples include walking away from the person you are cross with, taking a deep breath, counting to ten, and finding a quiet place to sit and think for a minute. Point out that all these ideas give us a chance to chill out and think about the situation more calmly. Often, when we think for a minute, our original cross reaction seems unjustified or silly.

Ask the children how they apologise to others if they have been cross. What do they say and do? Point out that it is never a good idea to stay cross for too long.

Provide the children with copies of photocopiable page 39 **Feeling cross** (core) or the extension version on the CD-ROM. At the end of the session, choose two or three children to explain their work to the rest of the class.

Activity 8: Conflict and resolution

Remind the children of the work they did in activity 7. Point out that when they felt cross they found lots of ways to help themselves calm down. Now ask them to think about times that they have argued with other children – for example, they might have argued over who owns something, disagreed on the rules of a game, or fallen out when someone broke something that belongs to them.

Ask the children to think of good ways of resolving a conflict and to explain their answers. Now talk about what bad ways there are of resolving conflicts. Place the children into four groups and give each group one of the **Conflict and resolution** cards. The children need to decide what the conflict might be and prepare a role play of a 'good' resolution to present to the rest of the class. Discuss each role play in turn and vote on the success of the resolution.

Now invite the children to try the **Good resolutions** interactive activity.

Extension
Encourage the children to write about a conflict they have had at home. How did they resolve it? Did they resolve it successfully? How could they have resolved it better?

Feelings

Activity 9 Being kind

Thank you for helping me when I hurt my arm.

Ajit

Ask the children what it means to be kind to someone. How do they feel if someone is kind to them? How do they feel when they are kind to someone else? What sorts of things have they done to be kind to someone at home, at school or in the community? Have they, for example, been kind to an elderly neighbour, or helped with charity work with their families?

Encourage the children to think of someone in the class who has been kind to them in some way. Select children to name someone who has been especially kind and to explain what the kindness was. Point out that this is a good opportunity to thank one another for their kindnesses.

Provide the children with copies of photocopiable page 40 **Being kind** (core) or the extension version on the CD-ROM to complete.

Extension
Invite the children to write a thank-you letter to someone who is always kind to them at home, at school or in the community.

Activity 10: Feeling frightened

Talk about the things that make us feel frightened. It may be scary TV programmes or stories, noises in the dark or an older child shouting in the playground. Encourage the children to tell the class about a time when they felt frightened.

Now ask the children to think about who helps them not to feel scared or frightened – a parent, carer, a friend or teacher perhaps. How do these people help them? What other ways are there that children can make themselves feel safe again? Where could they go? What could they do? For example, they could turn off the TV or change channel, take a favourite toy to bed with them for comfort, or go to a quiet place in school, such as the library.

Working individually, invite the children to try the **Feeling frightened** interactive activity.

Extension
Children can draw a rainbow and write different ways that they can stop themselves feeling scared or frightened on each strip.

Activity 11: Different feelings

Hand back the lists of feelings that the children completed in activity 1 **How do you feel?** Allow them a few minutes to read them through, then ask if they still agree with what they wrote. How have their opinions altered? What have they learned about feelings that they didn't know before?

Talk about how we can identify feelings in people. What clues can the children look for? Why do they think it is important to be able to recognise how other people are feeling?

Place the children into pairs – friendship pairs if possible. Provide each pair with two copies of the **My friend's feelings** template. Ask each partner in turn to complete the template after first finding out about their friend's feelings. At the end of the session, choose two or three pairs to share their findings with the others. Spend time discussing these findings. Display the sheets alongside other work from this unit.

Extension

Ask the children to write two or three sentences about how they could make members of their families happier at home. What could they do to help them? How could they be special friends to their siblings?

Activity 12: Thinking of others

Ask the children to reflect on all the work done in this unit. What is the most important thing they have learned about their own feelings and those of others?

Talk about putting ourselves in others' shoes. Ask the children to imagine what it must be like to fall over. Now ask them to imagine what it would be like to get a wonderful surprise. How would they feel? Point out that, although these things aren't happening to them right now, they can imagine how they, or others, would feel if they did.

Show the **Cartoon characters** illustrations on the whiteboard. Explain that cartoon characters show extremes of feelings or emotions so that the reader can put themselves into the character's shoes and enjoy the story even more. Place the children into groups and ask each group to select a cartoon character. They should decide how the character is feeling and make up a simple story to explain why the character is feeling this way. Ask each group to choose a scribe to jot down the outline of their story.

Invite the scribes to read out their stories. Do the others agree that the stories reflect the characters' feelings? Encourage the children to make alternative suggestions where appropriate.

Children can now complete the self-evaluation sheet and/or the children's booklet.

Feelings

My feelings

This is my happy face:

I feel happy when

_____

_____

_____

This is my cross face:

I feel cross when

_____

_____

_____

This is my sad face:

I feel sad when

_____

_____

_____

This is my frightened face:

I feel frightened when

_____

_____

_____

Feeling cross

Draw what makes you cross:

I feel cross when _____

_____

_____

Draw what you do to stop feeling cross:

To stop feeling cross I _____

_____

_____

Feelings

Being kind

Draw and label some of the people who are kind to you:

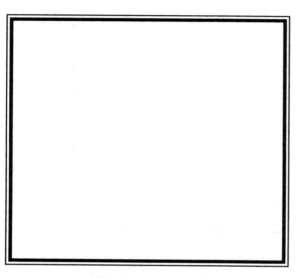

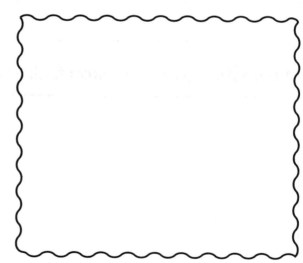

Help words

mum   dad   grandma   grandad   friend   sister
brother   aunt   uncle   carer   teacher   neighbour

What I've learned about feelings

Name _____

I often feel:

People show feelings in their faces. These people are:

_____   _____

_____   _____

I understand how people feel by _____

_____

I try to be kind and help others feel happier by _____

_____

Keeping healthy

Unit planner

Aims of the unit

Looking after our health is important to us all. Healthy lifestyles adopted in childhood lay firm foundations for future health. The aim of this unit is to develop the children's understanding of the steps they can take to maximise their chances of having a healthy life.

> **Key concept**
> Learning how we can keep our bodies healthy now and in the future.

Learning outcomes

By the end of this unit:
● All the children should be able to explain why it is important to lead a healthy lifestyle in order to keep healthy. They should be able to identify healthy and unhealthy foods. They should all be aware of the need for exercise in order to keep fit.
● Most should understand how to take care of their bodies by keeping them clean and free from infection. Most should also have a grasp of basic first aid for treating wounds.
● Some may be able to think constructively about keeping themselves healthy in the future and have some idea about how they will live and take care of themselves as adults to maintain optimum health.

Curriculum links

PSHE
● Developing a healthy, safer lifestyle
Every Child Matters
● Be healthy
SEAL themes
● Changes
PE
● Knowledge and understanding of fitness and health: pupils should be taught how important it is to be active; to recognise and describe how their bodies feel during different activities.
Science
● Humans and other animals: pupils should be taught that humans and other animals need food and water to stay alive; that taking exercise and eating the right types and amounts of food help humans to keep healthy; about the role of drugs as medicines.
Maths
● Processing, representing and interpreting data

> **Vocabulary**
> Healthy, health, unhealthy, hygiene, doctor, nurse, optician, dentist, inoculations, cough, sneeze, medicines

Keeping healthy

Organisation

The activities in this unit may be worked through in the order in which they appear or in any order to suit your ongoing planning. All of the activities are introduced as part of whole-class teaching. The follow-up activities include a range of individual, paired, small-group and whole-class work.

Resources

You will need the following resources to complete the activities in this unit:

Core photocopiable pages

Page 51 Keeping clean
Page 52 People who help us to stay healthy
Page 53 Noisy and quiet places
Page 54 Self-evaluation sheet

CD-ROM

Interactive activities:
● Healthy foods
● Bumps and bruises
● Healthy and unhealthy
Photocopiables:
● Keeping clean (support)
● Keeping clean (extension)
● People who help us to stay healthy (extension)
● Noisy and quiet places (support)
Plus core photocopiables as above

Photos:
Pets
Templates, cards and illuustrations:
● Healthy survey
● Food diary
● My health plan
Children's booklet:
Healthy me

Evaluation

The self-evaluation sheet and children's booklet have been designed to allow the children to assess how much they have learned about keeping healthy during this unit. It is suggested that the child responds to the evaluation by either drawing or writing answers according to his or her ability. Some guidance from an adult helper may be necessary.

Watch points

Be aware of the different lifestyles the children experience at home, especially their food choices. Remember that children may not have the choice to eat healthily at home. However, point out that, when eating school dinners, they can make healthier choices.

When visiting the first aid room in Activity 6 'Bumps and bruises' draw children's attention to the school health and safety guidelines. In the ensuing role-play stress the importance of wearing gloves when treating wounds at school and also to ascertain if the victim is allergic to anything e.g plasters or antiseptic cream. The interactive activity is set in a home context.

Keeping healthy

Let's talk

Circle time and thinking activities

These questions will get the children thinking and talking about keeping healthy. Ensure, before beginning the discussion, that the children understand what the word 'healthy' means. Encourage them to talk about what they know about healthy/unhealthy foods and lifestyles. This will give you a baseline of the children's knowledge on which you can build.

1 What does the word 'healthy' mean? How do you know if you are healthy? What happens if you become unhealthy? What things keep you healthy?

2 What do you know about healthy food? Do you know how much fruit and vegetables to eat in a day? How much do you eat at the moment?

3 What time do you go to bed? Do you think it is important to have enough sleep? How do you feel if you don't get enough? Do you sometimes find it hard to get to sleep?

4 How do you keep fit? Do you like doing sport? Which sports do you play? Do other people in your family do sport to keep fit? Which sports do they play?

5 Do you think it is important to keep clean? When do you wash your hands? Why is it important to wash your hands? Why is it important to wash your clothes? How do you feel if you don't wash your skin and your clothes?

6 Have you ever fallen over and hurt yourself? How did you feel? Who helped you? What did they do? What does a bruise look like?

7 Who looks after us when we are ill? When was the last time you had to stay at home because you were ill? Who looked after you? What did they do? How did you help yourself to get better?

8 How many of you have had to take medicine to get better? Who gave you the medicine? Where did it come from? Why should you never touch medicines that don't belong to you?

9 How many of you have pets? Do you look after your pets or does an adult help you? What jobs do you have to do? Why is it important to wash your hands after touching pets?

10 Do you think the playground is a noisy or a quiet place? What about the school library? Do you like being in noisy or quiet places? When do you like to be quiet? When do you like to be noisy?

Activities

Activity 1: Healthy me

What does it mean to be healthy? Ask the children to write down three sentences that summarise their ideas or to complete the first column in the chart on the self-evaluation sheet for this section. (Keep these lists for activity 11 **Healthy and unhealthy**.)

Point out that we need lots of things to keep us healthy. Display the **Healthy survey** template on the whiteboard. Ask the children to think about a typical day:
- What healthy food and drink do they have?
- What exercise do they do? (Include being out in the fresh air, doing jobs and so on.)
- What personal hygiene is part of each day?
- What rest and sleep do they get? (Include quite play and reading.)

Ask a volunteer to scribe some of these things on the whiteboard. Can the children add any things that they don't do every day, but do occasionally? Encourage the class to think of ways they could make their day healthier.

Children can them complete their own copy of the **Healthy survey** template. Display the sheets under the heading *This is what we do to keep healthy.*

Activity 2: Healthy food

Ask the children why they think it is important to eat healthy food. Does healthy food keep them fit and well? Take the opportunity to talk about junk food. Which junk foods do the children eat? How often? Why do they think these foods are called junk foods? How do they feel after eating them? Point out that junk food can be enjoyed occasionally, but it should not be eaten on a regular basis.

Encourage the children to think about the food they eat regularly. How many always have breakfast? Do they think it is important? How many never eat it? Explain that breakfast gives us energy to work in the morning.

Find out how many children have school lunches. What do they like/dislike about them? Invite the school cook to talk to the children about the sorts of foods he or she cooks and to explain how the menus are planned. Encourage the children to ask questions. If possible, arrange for the class to visit the cook in the school kitchens to see how their food is prepared.

Invite the children to help you sort foods into different groups using the **Healthy foods** interactive activity. Talk about the suggested number of portions of each food type.

Extension
Using the **Food diary** template, encourage the children to record how many servings of fruit and vegetables they eat.

Keeping healthy

Activity 3: Rest and sleep

Talk about the importance of having enough rest and sleep. Point out that the body repairs itself when we are asleep. Getting enough sleep is particularly important for children as it helps them grow.

Ask the children to draw two clocks – one showing the time they go to sleep and one showing the time they get up. How many hours' sleep do they have? Make a graph of the results for display. How many children have less than 10–11 hours sleep a night? Why is this so? (Some may be unaware how little sleep they actually get!) Do they feel tired the next day because of lack of sleep?

Identify times when the children find it hard to sleep – when they are excited before a birthday or Christmas perhaps? When do they find it easy to get to sleep? Examples might be when they have had a particularly tiring day with plenty of exercise. Ask the children to think about strategies for getting to sleep, such as reading and relaxing, having a warm drink and counting sheep.

Activity 4: Keeping fit

Discuss with the class why it is important to keep fit. What sorts of things do the children like to do to keep fit? Talk about the things they do each day – for example, they might walk or cycle to school, play with friends, or go to a sports club. What do they do at the weekend to keep fit – walk or cycle with their families, go swimming or dancing, fly a kite?

Talk about the sports that children play in and out of school. Place the children into groups and ask them to mime a sport for the others to guess.

Now ask the children how they feel after they have played sport. Do they feel happy, excited, tired? Do they feel better? Talk about the places they can go to play sport, such as leisure centres, swimming pools, or the school sports field. How many have used these facilities? What did they think about them?

With the class, compile information about the sports the children play both inside and outside of school. Ask the children to help you make a large block graph to display on the wall. Discuss your findings at the end of the session.

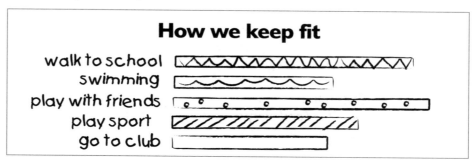

Activity 5: Personal hygiene

Spend time discussing with the children the importance of personal hygiene. Think of some important hygiene messages, such as cleaning your teeth regularly, being careful when you have a cold, putting tissues in the bin, and washing your hands.

Talk about the times in the day when the children should always wash their hands – for example, after using the toilet, before meals, after handling pets and after playing in the garden. Why is it important to wash at these times? What might happen if we don't? Explain that it is easy to spread germs if we don't wash our hands. Discuss other ways people can spread germs – for example, by not covering their noses when they sneeze or their mouths when they cough.

Point out to the children that we should all wash our bodies once a day. Ask them how they choose to wash – some may prefer to shower, some a bath, and some to wash at the basin. What other body washing do we do?

Give the children a copy of photocopiable page 51 **Keeping clean** (core), or the support or extension version on the CD-ROM and ask them to complete it.

Activity 6: Bumps and bruises

Ask the children if they have ever fallen over at school. Who helped them? What did this person do to make them feel more comfortable? Point out that everyone gets bumps and bruises at some time. Most need no treatment at all. Some cuts may need to be washed and dressed. Explain that some members of staff in school are specially trained to help children who get hurt.

Take the opportunity to visit the first aid room. What sorts of things are in the room? Some children may keep their medicines or inhalers there. Find out how many have been to the first aid room. What happened to them?

In the classroom, place children into groups and ask them to create a role play based on an accident in the playground. Children must choose who will play the victim, the child helper, the teacher on duty and the person who gives first aid. Allow time for them to practise and then encourage the groups to show their role plays to the rest of the class. Do the other children think they are accurate? How could they be improved?

Working in pairs, invite the children to complete the **Bumps and bruises** interactive activity. They can move the text and the pictures to put the tasks in the correct order, showing a parent or carer treating a cut at home. Discuss their choices in small groups; are there different ways to treat a cut?

Activity 7: People who look after our health

Talk about the people who help to keep us fit and well – the doctor, dentist, nurse and optician. Ask a child who has visited each person to describe what happened. Point out that these people don't only help to make us better when we are ill, they also help to keep us well and prevent some illnesses. Discuss the importance of having inoculations to prevent diseases, and regular check-ups with the dentist and optician.

Invite the school nurse to come into the classroom and tell the class about her work. Encourage the children to prepare questions in advance of her visit.

Ask the children to help you make a 'school clinic' in the corner of the classroom and encourage them to create role plays of the jobs done by doctors, nurses, opticians and dentists.

Children can now complete photocopiable page 52 **People who help us to stay healthy** (core) or the extension version on the CD-ROM.

Activity 8: Getting better

Find out how many of the children have been ill enough to have to stay in bed while they recover. What was wrong with them? How did they feel? How did other people, such as family members or carers, help them to get better? Did they make sure they got plenty of rest and drank plenty of water?

Talk about the role of medicines and show the children some example packets and bottles, if available. Find out how many children were given medicine when they were ill. Who gave them the medicine? Where did it come from? Take the opportunity to talk about the importance of not touching medicines – an adult must always give them medicine because it is important to have the right dose at the right time.

Do the children think it is important that people look after each other when they are ill? What could they do if someone in their family was ill?

Place the children into groups and ask each group to create a role play based on a time when they or a member of their family felt ill at home. Who looked after them? Choose groups to show their role plays to the rest of the class and discuss them together.

Keeping healthy

Activity 9: Our pets

Find out how many children have pets at home. Who looks after them? Who cleans their bedding, washes their food bowls, takes them for a walk? Display the **Pets** photos on the whiteboard as a prompt. Don't forget to discuss unusual pets!

Do the children think it is important to look after pets properly? Is it important to make sure they are kept clean? Why? Encourage them to share their own experiences of looking after pets. Extend the discussion by asking the children why we should wash our hands after handling pets.

Place the children into groups and ask them to design a poster entitled *Looking after a pet*, which should include a reminder for people to wash their hands after handling pets. They can download photos of pets from the CD-ROM to decorate their posters, or draw their own. Invite the children to vote on which is the most effective poster and display the winner in school.

Activity 10: Noisy and quiet places

Ask the children when they like to be quiet and when they like to make a lot of noise. Do they think it would be good to always have noise around us? Why/why not?

Encourage the children to describe the noisiest place they know. Is it a fun place to be? Why do they like/not like it? Do they like it sometimes? Now ask them to describe the place they like to go when they want to be quiet. Why do they go there? How do they feel after they have spent time there?

Take the children to a quiet place in school, such as the library corner. Ask them to describe the place. How do they feel when they are there? Can they concentrate better when there is no noise? Now invite them to observe the playground at playtime. What sort of noises can they hear? Is it exciting? Do some children find it worrying? How do they feel when they have had a noisy playtime?

Point out that we need both noisy and quiet places. Invite the children to complete photocopiable page 53 **Noisy and quiet places** (core) or the support version on the CD-ROM.

Noisy places

Quiet places

Keeping healthy

Activity 11: Healthy and unhealthy

Hand out the lists that the children completed at the start of activity 1 **Healthy me**. Allow them time to read through their sentences and encourage the children to reflect on what they have learned about keeping healthy. How have their opinions changed from the start of the unit? What do they think being healthy/unhealthy means now?

Ask the children to describe healthy and unhealthy lifestyles. Remind them to think about healthy food, taking enough exercise, avoiding spreading germs and getting enough rest. Highlight tasks from the activities to remind them what they have learned. What things can the children change in their own lives to keep them healthy now? What will they do in the future to make sure they lead healthy lifestyles when they are grown-up?

Working in pairs, invite the children to try the **Healthy and unhealthy** interactive activity. They must decide which things are healthy and which are unhealthy, and slot them into the appropriate boxes.

Children can now complete the self-evaluation sheet and/or the children's booklet.

Activity 12: Healthy views

Ask the children to reflect on all the work they have done in this unit. In their opinions, what is the most important thing they have learned about keeping healthy? Invite them to name one thing that they intend to do in future to help keep healthy. They can write a 'Health message' for the noticeboard as a reminder.

Encourage the children to use the **My health plan** template to help them formulate a plan to lead healthier lives. They should write bullet points under each heading. Invite them to show their work at the end of the session and to discuss their work with others. Come back to the plans in a month's time and review how many of the changes the children have been able to put into practice.

Extension
Ask the children to talk with their families about ways they could become healthier. Talk about the resolutions together the following day.

Keeping clean

Look at the children below. Write a sentence to show what you think they need to do next.

Keeping healthy

People who help us to stay healthy

Join the people with the things they use to help us keep fit and well.

Have you ever visited these people? Put a ✓ or a ✗ next to each one.

a doctor [ ]   an optician [ ]

a nurse [ ]   a dentist [ ]

Draw what happened at one visit on the back of this sheet.

Keeping healthy

Noisy and quiet places

Draw a quiet place here:

I like this quiet place because _____

_____

Now draw a noisy place:

I like this noisy place because

_____

_____

_____

Help words

think   fun   shout   read   daydream   listen   talk

share   exciting   rest   play   friends

Unit 3

Keeping healthy

What I've learned about being healthy

Name _____

Fill in the boxes to show what you have learned about having a healthy lifestyle.

	What I knew	What I've learned	What I'll change
Healthy food and drink			
Fitness			
Taking care of myself			

PHOTOCOPIABLE Health & Wellbeing ages 5-7

Unit planner

Aims of the unit

Keeping safe is important to everyone, especially children. Educating children to understand dangers without depriving them of the freedom to explore their surroundings is essential. The aim of this unit is to provide the children with the tools for keeping safe and the ability to assess risk in their everyday lives.

> **Key concept**
> Learning how to keep safe in different situations.

Learning outcomes

By the end of this unit:

- All the children should understand how to keep safe in familiar situations, such as in the home, at school and in the community. They should also understand why rules are made to keep people safe in these environments.
- Most should understand road safety rules and use them effectively. They should understand the importance of wearing protective clothing, such as bike helmets and reflective strips when cycling. They should also be able to name people they could ask for help if they are in danger or lost.
- Some may understand and be able to give reasons for the concept of individual responsibility to keep safe. Some may also be able to predict confidently what the consequences of their actions may be for themselves and others.

Curriculum links

PSHE
- Developing a healthy, safer lifestyle

Every Child Matters
- Stay safe

SEAL themes
- Say no to bullying

Geography
- Knowledge and understanding of patterns and processes: pupils should be taught to make observations about where things are located (for example, a pedestrian crossing).

Design and technology
- Working with tools, equipment, materials and components to make quality products: pupils should be taught to follow safe procedures for food safety and hygiene.

Science
- Health and safety: pupils should be taught to recognise that there are hazards in living things, materials and physical processes, and assess risks and take action to reduce risks to themselves and others.

> **Vocabulary**
> Safe, unsafe, accidents, safety, rules, bullies, secrets, risk

Unit 4

Keeping safe

Organisation

The activities in this unit may be worked through in the order in which they appear or in any order to suit your ongoing planning. All of the activities are introduced as part of whole-class teaching. The follow-up activities include a range of individual, paired, small-group and whole-class work.

Resources

You will need the following resources to complete the activities in this unit:

Core photocopiable pages
Page 64 Danger!
Page 65 Bullying is bad
Page 66 Secrets
Page 67 Self-evaluation sheet

CD-ROM

Interactive activities:
- Safe and unsafe places
- Emergency!
- Who can help?

Photocopiables:
- Danger! (support)
- The Green Cross Code
- Bullying is bad! (support)
- Bullying is bad! (extension)
- Secrets (extension)
Plus core photocopiables as above

Photos:
- Holiday dangers

Templates, cards and illustrations:
- Playground rules
- Safe people cards
- People I trust
- Keep safe rules

Children's booklet
- Keeping myself safe

Evaluation

The self-evaluation sheet and children's booklet have been designed to allow the children to assess how much they have learned about keeping safe during this unit. It is suggested that the child responds to the evaluation by either drawing or writing answers according to his or her ability. Some guidance from an adult helper may be necessary.

Watch points

Be aware of the different levels of childcare in homes. Be sensitive that some children may be more at risk of, for example, accidents at home, through a lack of parental supervision. However, remind all children that they can take steps to keep themselves safe by taking responsibility for their own safety.

When introducing Activity 6 'Accidents and emergencies' draw children's attention to the school fire and emergency procedures. Remind them that sometimes the procedures for these events are different depending if they are at school or at home. The interactive activity 'Emergency!' is set in a home context.

Let's talk

Circle time and thinking activities

These questions will get the children thinking and talking about keeping safe. Ensure, before beginning the discussion, that the children understand what the phrase 'keeping safe' means.

1 What does 'keeping safe' mean? What safe places can you think of? What is your favourite safe place? Why is it a safe place? Do you try to keep other people safe?

2 How do you keep safe at home? What things at home might be dangerous to you? Do you try to keep other people safe at home?

3 How do you keep safe at school? Can you think of a school rule that helps to keep you safe?

4 How many of you go away on holiday? Where have you visited on holiday? Was it a safe or an unsafe place? How could you tell? Have you ever got into danger on holiday? What happened?

5 How do you keep safe on the roads? Do you know how to cross the road safely? How do you keep safe on your bike? Where do you ride? What do you wear to keep safe?

6 What is an accident? Have you ever had an accident? What happened? What is an emergency? How would you get help in an emergency?

7 Have you ever felt unsafe at school? Have you ever been bullied? What happened? What did you do? Who did you tell? How did they help you?

8 Have you ever been lost? Where were you? Had you been there before? What happened? Who found you? How did you feel?

9 Can you keep a secret? What sort of secrets are you good at keeping? Why don't you tell these secrets? Is it always safe to keep a secret? Have you ever been told to keep a secret that you knew was bad? What happened?

10 What is a safe person? Which people do you think are safe people? Who would you ask to help you if you thought you were in danger? How can these people help you?

Activities

Activity 1: What is safe?

Ask the children what they think is safe – inside and outside. Collect and display some photos of safe and unsafe places and discuss them with the children. What things do they think are safe in the city and the country? Ask them to think of safe places they can go to. Examples might be at friends' homes, in school, with Grandma or at clubs they attend.

Remind the children that things can also be unsafe – for example, scissors and garden tools. Explore some other things that are sometimes not safe. Encourage all the children to participate in the discussion. Record their answers on tape to play back to them at the end of the unit during reflection time.

Working in pairs, invite the children to try the **Safe and unsafe places** interactive activity.

Extension
Ask the children how they would get help if they were in danger. For example, they could dial 999, ask a trusted neighbour for help, or speak to a teacher. Invite the children to write a simple plan of action they could refer to if they needed help. At the end of the session, encourage the class to share and discuss their plans with each other.

Activity 2: Keeping safe at home

Spend time talking with the children about the importance of keeping safe at home. Have any of them ever had an accident at home? What happened? How was the accident caused? Who helped them? Encourage the children to share their personal experiences with the class.

Now ask the children to think about their own homes. Which areas do they think might be the most dangerous? Why do they think these areas might be dangerous? Ask the children if there are rules they have to obey at home. They may not, for example, be allowed to play by the road, touch matches, or go near the oven. How do these rules help them to keep safe? What happens if they don't keep the rules?

Show photocopiable page 64 **Danger!** (core) on the whiteboard and discuss it with the class. Ask individuals to complete this sheet or the support version on the CD-ROM.

Stay away from fires   Don't play on the stairs   Take care in the garden

Activity 3: Keeping safe at school

Talk about keeping safe at school. How does your school try to keep people safe? What rules do the children know that help to keep them safe? Do they think the rules are good rules? Point out that the rules are designed to keep everybody safe. Ask them to tell you some safety rules. Examples might be not running in school and to always carry scissors with points down. Can the children recall having, or witnessing, an accident in school? What happened? Was the accident caused by someone breaking a school rule?

Using the whiteboard, ask the children to help you compose a list of classroom safety rules (or discuss a list that you already have). Talk about the children's suggestions and, where there is disagreement, take a vote on whether or not a particular rule is included.

Extension
Ask the children about playground rules. Do they think the rules already in place keep everyone safe? Encourage them to think about additional rules that would make the playground safer. Children can work in pairs and record their ideas on the **Playground rules** template. Display a selection of the lists near to the playground door.

Activity 4: Keeping safe on holiday

Ask the children where they have been on holiday. Did they stay in this country? Did they go abroad? Did they feel safe on holiday? Did their parents or carers impose rules on holiday? What were they? Were the rules made to keep them safe?

Do the children think it is important to be extra careful about keeping safe on holiday? Ask them to explain their answers.

Place the children into groups. Ask them to choose one person to act as a scribe. Now invite the groups each to choose a photo of a holiday scene from the **Holiday dangers** photos. Encourage them to talk about possible dangers in the scene and ask the scribes to make notes. At the end of the session, select members from each group to tell the others about their group's findings, using the notes to help them.

Extension
Ask children to complete the following sentence and illustrate it for a display: *On holiday I keep safe by...*

Activity 5: Keeping safe on the roads

Find out how many children know how to cross the road safely. How many know the Green Cross Code? What must we remember to do when crossing the road? Do the children know what pelican crossings, zebra crossings and crossing patrols are? How do these things help us to cross the road safely?

Invite the school crossing patrol warden or a local police officer into school to talk about crossing the road safely. Chalk a roadway and a pavement on the playground and encourage the children to demonstrate what they have learned.

Talk about keeping safe on the roads at night or when it is gloomy in the winter. Ask the children if they have reflective strips on their jackets. Point out that wearing something light-coloured also makes them more visible at night. Remind the children that they should always wear a bike helmet when cycling and wear their seatbelts in the car.

Invite the children to design an innovative piece of reflective clothing that they could wear to make them more visible on winter days. This could be reflective shoes, a badge, body bands and so on.

Extension
Ask the children to complete the **The Green Cross Code** photocopiable for homework.

Activity 6: Accidents and emergencies

Ask the children what an accident is. How many have had an accident? Were they badly hurt? What happened? Who helped them? Now ask them what an emergency is. What would they do, for example, if they saw a fire? Take the opportunity to remind them to get out of the building as fast as they can before they try and summon any help. What number should they dial to get the emergency services?

Have the children ever taken silly risks, perhaps encouraged to do so by older children or even their friends? What happened? Find out how many have decided not to do something silly even though their friends were prepared to take a risk.

Point out that accidents happen all the time and that often they can't be helped. But some things happen that are not accidents – for example, a child may deliberately push someone or hurt them. Remind the children that this is wrong. Ask the children to draw an accident and write a sentence about it. Encourage them to think about how it could have been avoided.

Talk to the children about the procedure they might follow if there was a fire at home. Then invite the children to try the **Emergency!** interactive activity and discuss their responses together.

Activity 7: Bullies

Ask the children if they know what a bully is. Who are bullies – other children, adults? Have they ever been bullied? Who did they ask for help? What happened? Take the opportunity to stress that bullying is not allowed in school. Make sure the children know who to ask for help if anyone should try and bully them.

Place the children into groups and ask them to create a role play explaining how they would deal with a bully. Suggest a different scenario for each group. For example:
- an older child trying to make a younger one do something bad like taking sweets from a shop
- bullying someone to take risks near dangerous places, such as a railway line or busy road
- taking money from a child and threatening to hurt them
- making personal comments.

Allow time for the children to practise their role plays before performing them in front of the others. Afterwards, talk about how each group dealt with the bully and stress the importance of different resolutions.

Encourage the children to complete photocopiable page 65 **Bullying is bad!** (core), or the support or extension version on the CD-ROM.

Activity 8: Getting lost

Talk to the children about getting lost. Ask them to think about the places they might get lost. How many of them have ever become separated from parents or family while they were out? What happened? Did they ask anyone for help? How did they get reunited with their family? How did they feel when they realised they were lost? How did they feel when they were found?

Talk about the people who can help us if we are lost. Remind the children only to approach people they can trust, such as a police officer. Find out how many can give accurate information about themselves in case they get lost – their full name, address and telephone number. Suggest that children who don't know this information should practise it with parents or carers at home.

Place the children into pairs and invite them to try the **Who can help?** interactive activity. Encourage the children to talk about each person and to justify their choices. Discuss their choices with the class and focus on how they make their choices.

Extension
Ask half the class to draw a picture of how they would feel if they were lost, and the other half to draw a picture of how they would feel when they were found. Display the drawings.

Activity 9: Don't tell!

Ask the children to tell you what a secret is. Have they ever kept a secret, such as not telling a brother or sister what they have bought them for a birthday present? Was this a good secret, a safe secret? Why? What are some other examples of good secrets?

Point out that some secrets are bad and that we do not have to keep bad secrets. Give the children an example, such as keeping it a secret that someone has stolen something or bullied someone. Ask the children if they can think of other secrets that are bad and that they should not keep. Point out that it is important to tell an adult they know and trust if they think a secret is a bad one, especially if they think they may be in danger. Talk about who these adults might be. Ask the children to think about the people they could tell about a bad secret.

Invite the children to complete photocopiable page 66 **Secrets** (core) or the extension version on the CD-ROM. At the end of the session, choose children to show their work to the others. Does everyone agree which secrets are safe and which are not?

Activity 10: Safe people

Talk about people the children know and trust well, such as their parents, carers and friends. Why do they feel safe with them? What other people do the children think are safe people? Examples may be the police, crossing patrol, teachers, teaching assistants, club leaders and so on. Encourage the children to explain why they feel safe with these people. On the whiteboard, make a list of all the people who children think keep them safe. Discuss each one as it is added to the list.

Cut up a copy of the **Safe people** cards and invite children to mime the people on the cards for the others to identify. Spend time discussing with the children why we trust these people.

Using the **People I trust** template on the CD-ROM, ask the children to choose five people they know and trust who they would go to if they needed help.

Safe people

Activity 11: Keep safe!

Spend time listening to the tapes you made of the children explaining what they thought was safe during activity 1 **What is safe?** Discuss what they said. What do they think is safe and unsafe now? Have their opinions altered or remained the same?

Ask the children to reflect about keeping safe in different places. What things will they bear in mind now that they have worked through the activities? Examples might be being more aware of dangers away from home; remembering to stay close to carers when on holiday; remembering who safe people are when asking for help, and so on. Encourage the children to think about what they have learned when answering.

Give the children a copy of the **Keep safe rules** template and encourage them to write down the most important rules they have learned, and the things they will watch out for from now on.

Activity 12: Is it safe?

Ask the children to reflect on all the work done in this unit. What is the most important thing they have learned about keeping safe? Ask them to name one thing they have learned that they intend to use in future to help keep them safe.

Remind them to think about possible consequences before doing something that might harm them. Give an example, such as if they play with matches, they might burn their fingers. Invite them to think of other things they might do that could have undesirable consequences. Point out that the children must be responsible for their actions and make sure they don't harm themselves or others.

Give pairs of children a potentially dangerous scenario and ask them to talk about it together and draw what they think will happen. For example:
- A small boy climbing a very high tree
- A girl stepping off the kerb without looking (a bicycle is coming)
- A child reaching for a boat in a pond
- A child carrying a pile of books who can't see an obstacle in his path.

Children can now complete the self-evaluation sheet and/or the children's booklet.

Keeping safe

Danger!

Look at this picture. Circle the things that are dangerous.

On the back of this sheet, draw what might happen in one situation.

Keeping safe

Bullying is bad!

Bullying is bad because:

● _____

  _____

● _____

  _____

● _____

  _____

● _____

  _____

● _____

  _____

Help words

mean   unkind   frighten   sad   lonely   nasty
dangerous   risks   younger   names

Keeping safe

Secrets

Look at these pictures and write **safe secret** or **unsafe secret** next to each one:

The big girl took my sweets. She said I must not tell my mum.

_____

Tom took money from Mum's purse. He said I must not tell her.

_____

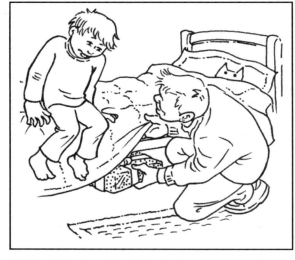

We hid Jack's birthday present. Dad said I must not tell him.

_____

Grandad bought flowers for Gran. He said I must not tell her.

_____

What I've learned about keeping safe

Name _____

Being safe on the road means:

_____

_____

_____

_____

Being safe at home means:

_____

_____

_____

The safe people I know are:

_____

_____

_____

_____

Being unsafe can:

_____

_____

_____

The difference between safe and unsafe is:

_____

_____

_____

Unit planner

Aims of the unit

Being able to establish and maintain good relationships is important at home, at school and in the wider community. Educating children how to maintain good relationships and to improve less harmonious ones through modifying their behaviour and developing mutual tolerance and understanding is vital for social harmony. The aim of this unit is to provide the children with the knowledge and understanding necessary to develop and keep good relationships.

> **Key concept**
> Establishing, maintaining and improving relationships.

Learning outcomes

By the end of this unit:

● All the children should understand what constitutes a good relationship and how they can maintain good relationships through respecting the differences between people and through moderating their own behaviour.

● Most should understand the diversity of relationships at home, at school and in the local community. They should also understand how to meet challenges in new situations, such as a new baby in the family, moving house or meeting step-parents.

● Some should develop a wider understanding of the impact of culture on relationships in the community and at school. They should have some knowledge of the need for mutual understanding and acceptance of others' beliefs and lifestyles.

Curriculum links

PSHE
● Developing good relationships and respecting the differences between people
Every Child Matters
● Make a positive contribution
SEAL themes
● Getting on and falling out
● Say no to bullying
● Relationships
Science
● Variation and classification: pupils should be taught to recognise the similarities and differences between themselves and others, and to treat others with sensitivity.

> **Vocabulary**
> Relationships, families, behaviour, care, share, tease, bullying, understanding, culture, celebrate

Organisation

The activities in this unit may be worked through in the order in which they appear or in any order to suit your ongoing planning. All of the activities are introduced as part of whole-class teaching. The follow-up activities include a range of individual, paired, small-group and whole-class work.

Resources
You will need the following resources to complete the activities in this unit:

Core photocopiable pages
Page 77 My relationships
Page 78 Teasing and bullying
Page 79 Saying goodbye
Page 80 Self-evaluation sheet

CD-ROM

Interactive activities:
● Caring and sharing
● Moving on
● Let's celebrate!

Photocopiables:
● My relationships (support)
● Teasing and bullying (support)
● Teasing and bullying (extension)
● Saying goodbye (support)
Plus core photocopiables as above

Photos:
● Clothes
● Celebrations

Templates, cards and illustrations:
● Behaviour and relationships
● Eating together
● Traditional clothes
● Good friendship rules

Children's booklet:
● My relationships

Evaluation
The self-evaluation sheet and children's booklet have been designed to allow the children to assess how much they have learned about developing good relationships during this unit. It is suggested that the child responds to the evaluation by either drawing or writing answers according to his or her ability. Some guidance from an adult helper may be necessary.

Watch points
Be aware of the different and complex relationships in some families. Similarly, be aware that some children may currently be experiencing difficulties at home through divorce or bereavement, for example, and that some issues in this unit (such as in activity 2 **Extended families** and activity 9 **Moving house**) may need to be handled particularly sensitively.

Good relationships

Let's talk

Circle time and thinking activities

These questions will get the children thinking and talking about forging and maintaining good relationships. Ensure, before beginning the discussion, that the children understand what the word 'relationship' means.

1 Who are your relations? What sort of relationships do you have with your family/carers? Do you always get along with them? Do you sometimes argue? What about? Do you think your behaviour affects other people in the family?

2 How many of you have step-brothers and step-sisters? Do they like the same things as you? Do you get on well with them? How do you behave when you are with your step-families?

3 Are you well behaved at school? Do you behave differently at home than in school? Do you think it is important to behave well? Why?

4 Is everyone in this classroom the same? What do we have in common? How are we different? Do we all look the same? Do we all like the same things? Do we all eat the same foods? Do we all wear the same clothes?

5 What does it mean to care about someone? What do you do to show you care for others? What do you and your family do to care for others? Do you know anyone who is disabled? How could show you care for someone who is disabled?

6 What is the difference between bullying and teasing? How many of you are teased at home? Do you mind being teased? Have any of you been bullied?

7 Do you know people from different cultures in the community? Have you eaten meals with them? What did you eat? Did you like it? What is good about knowing people from different cultures?

8 Do you think it is important to understand what other people are thinking or feeling? Why? How could you understand other people more?

9 How many of you have moved house? How did you feel? What things were you worried about? What things were you excited about?

10 What do you like to celebrate? Why do you like to celebrate these occasions? What is your favourite occasion?

Activities

Activity 1: Relationships

Ensure the children understand the meaning of the word 'relationship'. Record onto tape their views on their relationships at home. Extend this to asking them to talk about the relationships they have with friends, neighbours and sitters (if they have them). How are these relationships different? Are they polite to neighbours, for example? Do they have a more relaxed relationship with friends, say, than with their own brothers and sisters? (Keep the recordings to refer to later in activity 11 **Relationships are important**.)

Point out that we form different relationships with lots of people. We can be sons, daughters, neighbours and friends. We form relationships with friends in school, with people outside school and with our families. We even form relationships in the community with neighbours, club members and people with whom we take part in activities.

Give the children a copy of photocopiable page 77 **My relationships** (core) or the support version on the CD-ROM and ask them to identify the different relationships they have.

Extension
If appropriate, invite the children to draw their family trees with the help of parents, grandparents and other family members at home.

Activity 2: Extended families

Remind the children of the work you did in activity 1. Now ask them to think about their extended families. These may include people such as cousins, aunts, uncles and grandparents. They may also include carers, step-parents and step-brothers and sisters. Find out how many regularly see, for example, their grandparents. What sort of relationship do they have with them? Are they, perhaps, a little shy of them because they don't see them often? Do they think it is important to see each other a lot to keep a good relationship going? Encourage the children to share their personal experiences.

Now ask the children if they have step-parents and step-brothers and sisters. How often do they see them? Do they get on well with them? Encourage the children to give reasons for their answers. How do the children think they can improve relationships with their extended families?

Ask the children to draw a picture of someone in their extended family, and write two or three sentences explaining who they are and how they feel about them.

Activity 3: Behaviour and relationships

Begin this activity by talking about the children's behaviour in school. Why do the children think it is important to behave well? What happens if they don't? How does it feel in class when everyone behaves well? Is it easier to work? Extend this by talking about their behaviour outside. Do the children think it is important to behave outside in the community? Have they seen people behaving badly in the street? What did they see? How did they feel?

Now ask the children how they behave at home. Do they think they generally behave well? What happens if they misbehave? Have any of the children found it difficult to behave well – for example, when meeting a new baby brother or sister, or a new step-dad or step-mum, for the first time? What happened?

Place the children into four groups. Cut up a copy of the **Behaviour and relationships** cards and give each group a card. Ask the children to create a role play of the scenario to show how bad behaviour might affect relationships. Allow time for the groups to practise and then invite them to perform for the rest of the class. Discuss how the behaviour could be improved in each scenario to improve relationships in the family.

Extension
Give the children one card each and ask them to write something positive they could say in the situation.

Activity 4: Being the same, being different

Ask the children if everyone in class is good at the same thing. Is everyone good at art? Is everyone good at football? Point out that we have lots of things in common but everyone is different – emphasise how boring it would be if we weren't!

Now ask the children to think about people in the community. Is everyone able-bodied? Encourage the class to think what it must be like, for example, not to be able to see or hear, or to use a wheelchair. (Be sensitive to children in your school with disabilities during this discussion.)

Take the children into the playground and place them into pairs. Blindfold one child in each pair and ask the 'sighted' child to help the blindfolded child move around. After a few minutes, ask them to swap and repeat the process. Back in the classroom, discuss the activity. How did the children feel when they were blindfolded? How did the helpers feel? Did they feel responsible for the other's safety? Take the opportunity to point out that we all have different strengths and weaknesses, but that we should be ready to help people less able than ourselves. Everyone deserves respect.

Activity 5: Caring and sharing

Talk to the children about caring for others and sharing with them. What does it mean to care for someone or something? How do we show we care? Who do the children care about in school or at home? Who do the children share with? What sorts of things do they share both at home and at school? Do they think it is important to care for others and to share what we have? Ask them to give reasons for their answers.

Now talk about who we might care for in the community – our neighbours or elderly people, for example. How do we care for them? What things might we share with them? (Our time, friendship, food.) Do the children or their families care for anyone in the community? What do they do? What things do they share?

How do we care for people in other countries? Can the children think of examples where the school community has shown that it cared? You may wish to show the children a charity website such as Oxfam or Christian Aid to see how people care for others in times of crisis.

Invite the children to try the **Caring and sharing** interactive activity. Ask them to work in pairs and discuss their choices.

Activity 6: Teasing and bullying

Ask the children what teasing is. Does anyone at home or school tease them? How? Does it make them laugh? Is it meant to make them laugh? Now talk about bullying. What is bullying? Is it meant to make them laugh or not? Invite the children to talk about a time when they may have been bullied. Remind them that bullying is not allowed and must always be reported to an adult they know and trust.

Talk about the sorts of things bullies might do, such as demanding money, hurting others, or calling others spiteful names. Discuss what steps the children could take to protect themselves from bullies.

Place the children into four groups. Ask two groups to role play children who are teasing each other, and two to role play examples of bullying. (Remind the children in the bullying groups not to hurt each other, but just to act out what they think might happen.) Allow time for the groups to practise and then encourage them to perform for the rest of the class. Spend time discussing the performances. Highlight features of teasing and bullying and encourage the children to identify the differences.

Working in pairs, ask the children to complete photocopiable page 78 **Teasing and bullying** (core), or the support or extension version on the CD-ROM.

Activity 7: Eating together

In preparation for this activity, ask the children to talk about when they eat together with their families or friends. What special celebrations do they enjoy with their families or with the community where they eat together? Examples might be birthdays (their own or special birthdays for others, such as Grandma's 80th), Christmas, Diwali, Passover and so on. Encourage the children to tell the others what they eat at these special occasions.

If possible, invite people from different cultural or religious groups to come into the classroom to explain and show the foods that they eat as part of a special festival. Encourage the children to try some of the foods.

Give out copies of the *Eating together* template and ask the children to choose a special event. They can write who would join them on the chairs and decorate the table.

Extension

Provide the children with paper plates. Ask them to draw their favourite celebration meals that they enjoy with their families. At the end of the session, encourage them to tell the others what their meals contain. How many like the same foods? Who likes different foods?

Activity 8: Understanding others

Use this activity as a follow-up to activity 7. Point out that people from different cultures often eat different foods and that sometimes certain foods are not eaten at all. Find out from the children if there are foods they are not allowed to eat. What foods are they?

Show the children the children the *Clothes* photos or talk about the clothes worn by the children and adults in your school and the clothes (national dress and traditional) worn in the photos. Highlight the importance of different types of clothes to different cultures and encourage the children to appreciate why they are worn. If possible, provide the children with a selection of clothes from other cultures to try on. Point out that we should respect people from different cultures who may wear clothes that are different from ours.

Using the *Traditional clothes* template, invite the children to draw themselves in the mirror in an outfit they have seen others wearing. If they have tried on the clothes, they can write a sentence describing how they felt.

Activity 9: Moving on

Ask the children to talk about how they felt when they had to move somewhere new – to another class, another school, a new town or even overseas. Did they move a long way? Did they have to go to a new school? How easy was it to make new friends? How hard was it to leave old friends behind? How do they communicate with their friends now?

Spend time thinking about the challenges that arise when moving on. Point out that the children have to be quite bold to make new friends, for example, or to join new clubs. Encourage them to think of other challenges that arise at these times.

Invite the children, in pairs, to try the **Moving on** interactive activity. Ask them to discuss each situation and how it feels, and to think about the most appropriate way to stay in touch. Are there other ways to stay in touch?

Give each child a copy of photocopiable page 79 **Saying goodbye** (core) or the support version on the CD-ROM. The children can either draw on their own experiences or imagine what it must feel like to move away from a best friend. Choose two or three children to share their work. Find out if the others agree or disagree with the opinions expressed.

Activity 10: Let's celebrate!

Display the **Celebrations** photos on the whiteboard and discuss them with the class. Ask the children to bring in photos of them celebrating an event with their family or in the community. Encourage them to describe what the event was and who they shared it with. Make a display with captions that explain the relationships of those celebrating – for example, *I celebrated my Nan's birthday with my family.*

Invite the children to talk about special celebrations that they enjoy with their families and friends – for example, birthday parties, weddings and baptisms. Find out how they celebrate these occasions. Who do they celebrate with? Do they enjoy sharing the celebrations? What do they do? Now ask the children what celebrations they enjoy within the community – Bonfire Night, Diwali, Eid, carol concerts and so on. Once again, encourage the children to share their personal experiences with the others.

Invite the children to try the **Let's celebrate!** interactive activity.

Extension
Arrange for the children to take part in a class 'wedding' or other event. They can vote for the children who will play bride, groom and attendants. Make sure everyone knows their relationships in the event. Help the children to write invitation cards and prepare some simple party food for the reception. Invite parents, helpers and carers to join in the fun. Afterwards, encourage the children to talk about the celebration. Did they enjoy it?

Activity 11: Relationships are important

Play back the recordings you made of the children's opinions of what good relationships are from activity 1, **Relationships.** Do the children still agree with what they said? How have their opinions altered? What have they learned about keeping and improving relationships? Have they tried to improve their relationships with people, such as their family and friends? Have they tried to improve their relationships in the wider community with friends and neighbours? What did they do?

Ask the children which 'rules' they think are important when making good relationships. Write their ideas on the whiteboard. At the end of the session, read through the rules together. Encourage the children to think about how they can follow them in the future.

Using the **Good friendship rules** template, ask the children to write their own rules for maintaining good relationships. Choose two or three children to share their work with the others. Did any children write the same rules? How many thought other rules were more important?

Activity 12: Improving relationships

Ask the children to reflect on all the work done in this unit. What is the most important thing they have learned about making and keeping good relationships? Encourage the class to discuss what they have learned about improving relationships. How can they modify their own behaviour to improve relationships with others – at home, at school and in the wider community?

Tell the class that everyone is going to write a promise to do something to improve their relationships with others. Make a class list of ideas to help get them started. For example, *I will be kind to my little sister. I will share my toys with Tom. I won't play football near my neighbour's fence.*

Ask each child to write their name and their promise on a piece of card. Remind them to check their work for spelling and punctuation accuracy. They can then help you to create a display entitled *Our good relationship promises.*

Children can now complete the self-evaluation sheet and/or the children's booklet.

My relationships

Draw people in your pyramid.

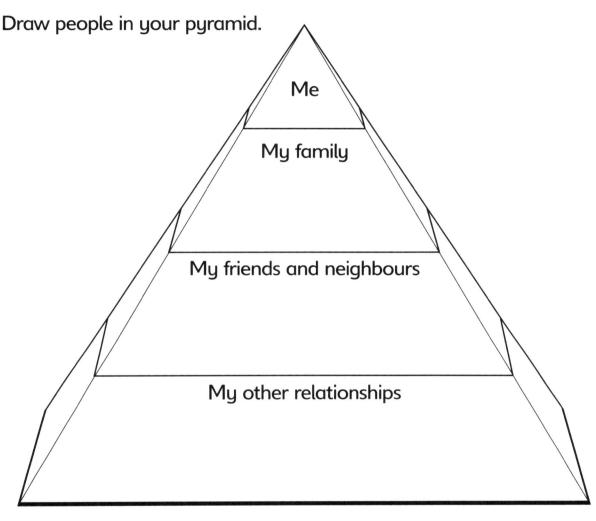

Me

My family

My friends and neighbours

My other relationships

Write your name _____

Who are you? Circle the right labels.

a son   a daughter   a neighbour   a friend   a sister   a brother

Write the labels.

I am ...

● _____   ● _____

Good relationships

Teasing and bullying

What would you say to the bully? Write what you would say:

Give me your sweets, now!

_____

_____

_____

Saying goodbye

Kelly lives next door to Sam.
Kelly and Sam are best friends.

But Kelly is moving house.

How does she feel? _____

_____

How does Sam feel? _____

_____

How can Sam and Kelly stay friends? _____

_____

_____

Draw Sam and Kelly staying friends.

Good relationships

What I've learned about relationships

Name _____

I have relationships with lots of different people – my family, friends and neighbours. Some people are like me and some people are different from me. This is a picture of one of my friends:

I am friends with _____ because _____

_____

To make new friends I _____

_____

To stay friends I _____

_____

To help people I _____

_____

Health & Wellbeing ages 5-7

Unit planner

Aims of the unit

Looking after the environment is probably the most important challenge we face. Everyone can make changes to their everyday lives to help protect the environment in some way. Small steps such as using our cars less and recycling our rubbish can all make significant differences. This unit aims to help children understand the importance of making these changes and encourages them to behave as responsible members of the community.

> **Key concept**
> Understanding why and how we should look after the community and the environment.

Learning outcomes

By the end of this unit:
● All the children should be able to explain why it is important to protect the community and the environment. They should be able to identify common causes of pollution in the local area (including their school), such as litter and vehicle fumes.
● Most should understand the basic concepts of recycling and reusing materials to save energy and resources.
● Some may be able to generate new ideas both for looking after the community and the environment and ways of encouraging others to do the same.

Curriculum links

PSHE
● Preparing to play an active role as citizens
Every Child Matters
● Make a positive contribution
SEAL themes
● Changes
Geography
● Geographical enquiry and skills: pupils should be taught to ask geographical questions; observe and record; express their own views about people, places and environments; communicate in different ways.

> **Vocabulary**
> Environment, community, local, school, homes, pollution, recycling, wildlife, property

Organisation

The activities in this unit may be worked through in the order in which they appear or in any order to suit your ongoing planning. All of the activities are introduced as part of whole-class teaching. The follow-up activities include a range of individual, paired, small-group and whole-class work.

Looking after our environment

Resources
You will need the following resources to complete the activities in this unit:

Core photocopiable pages
Page 90 Let's clean up
Page 91 My report
Page 92 Respect!
Page 93 Self-evaluation sheet

CD-ROM
Interactive activities:
- Tidy up!
- Recycling bins
- Green spaces

Photocopiables:
- Let's clean up (support)
- Let's clean up (extension)
- My report (extension)
- Respect! (extension)
Plus core photocopiables as above

Templates, cards and illustrations:
- Being responsible
- Who's responsible?
- I can help
- My plan

Children's booklet:
- Looking after our environment

Evaluation
The self-evaluation sheet and children's booklet have been designed to allow the children to assess how much they have learned about looking after the environment during this unit. It is suggested that the child responds to the evaluation by either drawing or writing answers according to his or her ability. Some guidance from an adult helper may be necessary.

Watch points
Be aware of the different types of homes in which children may live. Avoid criticising untidy or dirty homes, but encourage the children to take positive steps to improve their own environments.

Let's talk

Circle time and thinking activities

These questions will get the children thinking and talking about how they can look after their community and the environment. Ensure, before beginning the discussion, that the children understand the words 'community' and 'environment'. Encourage them to think about their home environment first before extending the discussion to thinking about the local area and, if appropriate for the maturity of the class, the world environment.

1 What is a community? How many communities are you part of? What is the local community? What do you like about living in a community? What is the environment? What other environments are there?

2 Do you think it is important to look after your home? Why? What would your home be like if you didn't look after it? How do you help look after your home?

3 How do we look after our school? Who keeps the school clean for us? Who looks after the grounds? How can you help to look after our school? Is it important to look after our school? Why?

4 How many of you live near school? How many live further away? What is it like where you live? What are the best things about where you live? What are the worst things? How could you help to look after where you live?

5 What do you know about pollution? Is it a good or bad thing? Why? What pollutes our streets? What pollutes the rivers? What could you do to help stop pollution?

6 How many of you recycle at home? What things do you recycle? Why is it good to recycle? How do we recycle things at school?

7 Have you ever made something new from something old? What did you make? Were you pleased with what you made?

8 Do you or your families care for wildlife? What do you do? How many of you put food out for the birds in winter? Why is this a good thing to do? How else could you care for wildlife?

9 Can you think of any green spaces near school? Have you visited these places? What are they like? What do you do there? How do you look after these green spaces?

10 Do you always remember to ask if you want to borrow something from a friend? Is it important to do this? Why? How do you feel if someone takes something of yours without asking?

Activities

Activity 1: The community and the environment

Talk about the words 'community' and 'environment'. What do they mean? Invite the children to write down their ideas or to complete the first column in the chart on the self-evaluation sheet for this section. (Keep these notes to use in activity 11 **Make a difference!**)

Ask the children to describe how they can take care of their environment. How are they responsible for their environment at home? Do they keep their rooms tidy and help with jobs, such as recycling and collecting leaves? Now talk about the school environment. Can the children think of things they can do to improve the environment at school? For example, they can keep the classroom tidy and not drop litter in the playground. Why is it important to do these things?

Can the class think of important things that we all have to do to care for our communities? Ask the children to write the most important community issue they can think of on a leaf-shaped piece of paper and create a classroom tree display.

Give each child a copy of photocopiable page 90 **Let's clean up** (core), or the support or extension version on the CD-ROM to complete.

Activity 2: My home environment

Talk about how we take care of our home environments. Find out how many children help at home. How many are expected to take care of their own things and keep their rooms tidy? What other things are the children responsible for looking after at home? How many help with jobs that improve the home environment, such as sorting recycling, helping in the garden or refilling the bird feeder?

Place the children into pairs to work on the **Tidy up!** interactive activity.

Cut up a copy of the **Being responsible** cards and place the children into small groups. Invite each group to choose a card and to create a role play of the scenario. Allow the children a few minutes to practise, then call them together and invite some groups to show their role plays to the others. How do these actions affect the environment?

Activity 3: My school environment

Talk about why it is important to look after the school environment. Who is responsible for keeping the school clean and tidy? Is it just the cleaners' job or should everyone help? What things do the children appreciate about a tidy school? For example, it's nice to sit in clean classrooms and not to have litter in the playground. What would school be like if no one looked after it? Encourage all the children to participate in the discussion.

At playtime, invite the children to observe how other children in school use the playground. Do they all respect the area? Are some children harming the environment? They may spot children dropping paper or food, or not respecting trees or plants in the school grounds.

Show children the **Who's responsible?** template on the whiteboard, and ask them to think about the questions as you walk around the school. Observe busy areas such as the cloakrooms, washrooms, dining hall and so on. Ask them to look for anything that makes the school environment untidy or dirty.

Back in the classroom, spend time talking about what the children have observed then encourage them to complete their own copy of the **Who's responsible?** template.

Activity 4: The local environment

Talk about the area immediately surrounding the school. Is it a good environment? Who is responsible for keeping it clean and tidy? Encourage the children to give reasons for their answers.

If possible, take the children on a fact-finding walk around the local area to assess its general level of upkeep. Try to find examples of clean and dirty areas.

Ask the children what they discovered from their walk. What was good about the environment? What was not? Who might be responsible for clearing up litter? What other things need to be done to create a good environment?

Give the children a copy of photocopiable page 91 **My report** (core) or the extension version on the CD-ROM. This is a scaffolded activity to help the children write up their findings. At the end of the session, invite the children to share their reports with the others and to discuss their findings.

Looking after our environment

Activity 5: Pollution

Talk about the problem of pollution. Give the children a simple definition of the word 'pollution' – for example, *Things that make our environment dirty or dangerous.* Ask them to think back to the work you did in activity 3. Point out that one of the main problems was the litter and the objects left lying around that made the school look untidy.

Now ask the children to think about other environments other than school. What sorts of pollution cause problems in towns? For example – litter, traffic noise and fumes, factory smoke.

Can the children think of ways to help reduce pollution in towns? For example, they could take their litter home with them and use environmentally friendly ways of travelling to school, such as walking, creating a walking bus, taking public transport or riding a bike. List the children's ideas on the board and invite them to vote on one they think they should do to help the environment.

Extension
Using the **I can help** template, encourage the children to write down three things they could do to help reduce pollution.

Activity 6: Recycling

Before you do this activity, collect information from your local council about the recycling services available in your area.

Find out what the children understand by recycling. Do they recycle things at home? Why do they think recycling is important?

Working in groups, let the children look through the information you have gathered. Try to arrange the groups to include a competent reader in each. Discuss what each group has found out.

Now invite small groups of children to complete the **Recycling bins** interactive activity. They need to sort the items of rubbish into the correct recycling bins.

Extension
Set up a series of bins in your classroom and collect materials for recycling and composting.

Activity 7: New from old

Before you do this activity, collect items (or pictures of items) that have been made from recycled goods. For example – greetings cards made from recycled paper, recycled plastic carrier bags, pencils made from vending machine cups, and fleece jackets made from recycled plastic. Talk about each one with the class.

Ask the children why they think it is important to recycle things in this way. You can also talk about how things such as carrier bags do not have to be thrown away after one use, but can be reused again and again.

Point out that, in school, things are often recycled or reused. For example, children may use scrap paper to write notes, or use old cardboard in art lessons. Place the children into pairs or small groups and ask them to create a 'rubbish monster' using a selection of cartons, boxes, yogurt pots and cardboard. Encourage them to think of names for their monsters and to make name labels.

Activity 8: Caring for wildlife

Before you do this activity, visit the WWF and RSPB websites and familiarise yourself with the content. Display the websites on the whiteboard or allow the children to investigate them in small groups. Spend time ensuring that the children understand what wildlife is and talk about wildlife they have observed in your local area.

Discuss the importance of caring for wildlife. What do the children think would happen if our wildlife disappeared? Why do they think some wildlife is in danger? Can the children think of any local areas where pollution has harmed wildlife? Encourage all the children to give their opinions.

Look at the websites again and talk about how charities raise awareness of the problems facing wild animals and plants. Working in pairs, invite the children to design a poster that tells people how to look after wildlife – for example, by not dropping litter that could be harmful or by putting out food for wild birds.

Caring for animals

Looking after our environment

Activity 9: Green spaces

Arrange a visit to a local beauty spot or park. Remind the children that trees and green spaces are important as they help to reduce air pollution. Encourage the children to make notes about or draw pictures of the places they like best.

Back in the classroom, ask the children to talk about what they have seen. They can refer to their notes or drawings to help them remember. Now ask them to think about what they could do to look after green spaces. For example, they could put their litter in the bin, keep off flowerbeds in the park, and be careful not to damage gates and fences in the countryside.

In pairs, ask the children to complete the **Green spaces** interactive activity. This involves highlighting examples of people caring for and damaging green spaces.

Activity 10: Respecting the environment

Ask the children how they feel if someone damages something that belongs to them, such as a favourite toy. Do any of them have younger brothers and sisters who have ever broken anything of theirs? How did they feel?

Now talk about respecting the community property, such as parks, ponds, the seaside and the environment. Why do the children think it is important to respect these things?

Look at photocopiable page 92 **Respect!** on the whiteboard and talk about what is happening in the pictures. Now place the children into groups and ask them to create role-play scenarios where children are damaging community property or the environment. One person in each group should play the role of the owner of the property. Allow time for the children to practise their role plays before they perform them to the rest of the class.

Invite the children to complete photocopiable page 92 **Respect!** (core) or the extension version on the CD-ROM.

Looking after our environment

Activity 11: Make a difference!

Hand out the lists of ideas that the children wrote in activity 1 **The community and the environment.** Allow them time to re-read what they wrote and encourage them to reflect on what they have learned since then. What did they think before? What do they think now?

Take the opportunity to point out that everyone can make a difference to the welfare of the environment. Tell the children that they are all going to make a five-point plan. to help them remember to look after the environment. To get them started, write a class list of ideas – for example, *Always put litter in the bin; Don't hurt animals or damage plants.*

Using the **My plan** template, ask the children to write or draw five things they should remember about looking after the environment.

Children can now complete the self-evaluation sheet and/or the children's booklet.

Activity 12: All views considered

Ask the children to reflect on all the work done in this unit. What is the most important thing they have learned? Children could ask members of the School Council to come and talk to them about how they deal with environmental issues in the school and its surroundings. Encourage the children to tell council members of any concerns they have after the research they have carried out during the unit.

Ask the children to give their views on what the biggest dangers to the environment are. Ensure that everyone listens politely while others express their opinions, and encourage discussion and debate.

Remind the children that they can choose whether or not to look after the environment, but that there are consequences if they don't. Invite the children to give some examples – for example, *If we don't throw litter away properly, it may harm animals.*

Looking after our environment

Let's clean up

What do you need to help you clean these things? Cut out the word cards and stick them in the correct places.

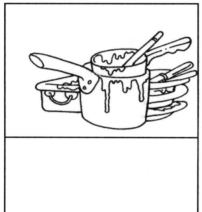

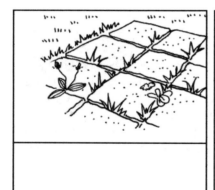

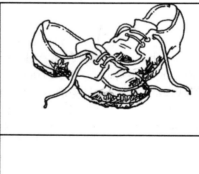

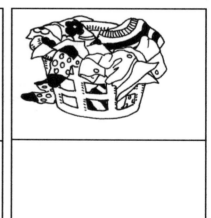

bin bag

washing-up liquid

shoe polish

washing powder

hoe

mop and bucket

My report

Draw a picture of the place.

Is this a clean or dirty place? Why? _____

. _____

_____

_____

How could you make it cleaner? _____

_____

_____

Who could help you? _____

_____

Help words
street   road   litter   rubbish   newspapers   bins
pollution   neighbours   friends   sweep

Looking after our environment

Respect!

Write what the children should say in the speech bubbles.
You can use these words:

Sorry	We won't do it again	We'll put it back
	We'll help plant some more	

Are the children showing respect for the environment? _____

_____

Is this good or bad for the environment? _____

_____

Our environment

Name _____

Fill in the boxes to show what you have learned about our environment.

	What I knew	What I've learned	What I'll change
The local environment			
The importance of protecting the environment			
Causes of pollution			
How to improve the environment			

![SCHOLASTIC]

Also available in this series:

ISBN 978-1407-10020-3

ISBN 978-1407-10021-0

ISBN 978-1407-10022-7

ISBN 978-1407-10023-4

Also available for Scotland:

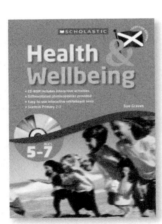

ISBN 978-1407-10024-1

ISBN 978-1407-10025-8

ISBN 978-1407-10026-5

ISBN 978-1407-10027-2

To find out more, call: 0845 603 9091
or visit our website www.scholastic.co.uk